STUDENT'S BOOK

English Explorer 3

Helen Stephenson
Jane Bailey

NATIONAL GEOGRAPHIC LEARNING | CENGAGE Learning

Australia • Brazil • Japan • Korea • Mexico • Singapore • Spain • United Kingdom • United States

Contents

Skills: Listening & Speaking	Working with words Study Skills Pronunciation	Culture & CLIL
Listening: A student talking about her school **Speaking:** Making greetings and introductions	**Working with words:** positive adjective - negative adjective *do* and *make* **Study skills:** using pictures **Pronunciation:** stressed forms and weak forms	**Reading:** Australia online: The world's largest classroom **Listening:** A teacher talking about his school **CLIL:** Technology and English Languages and the Internet
Listening: A biography of a musician **Speaking:** Asking for information on the phone	**Working with words:** nouns – adjectives nouns and verbs – nouns **Study skills:** topic words **Pronunciation:** the sounds /t/ and /d/ before /j/	**Reading:** British artists **Listening:** People's opinions of an artist's work **CLIL:** Art and English Vincent van Gogh
Listening: A radio programme about Lance Armstrong **Speaking:** Agreeing and disagreeing	**Working with words:** noun + noun adjective + preposition **Study skills:** predict and check **Pronunciation:** vowel sounds /æ/ and /ʌ/ in irregular verbs	**Reading:** Staying healthy in Africa **Listening:** The *Malaria No More* campaign **CLIL:** Biology and English Blood groups
Listening: An interview about animals **Speaking:** Giving and checking information	**Working with words:** adjective + noun false friends **Study skills:** similar words **Pronunciation:** the letter 'o' and 'oo', and the vowel sounds /u/, /uː/ and /ʌ/	**Reading:** Animals in India **Listening:** A journalist talking about elephants **CLIL:** Biology and English Endangered species
Listening: A Chinese-American student talking about China **Speaking:** Talking about problems	**Working with words:** compound adjectives phrasal verbs for relationships **Study skills:** specific information **Pronunciation:** homonyms with the sound /eə/	**Reading:** Multicultural Canada **Listening:** A chat-show programme **CLIL:** History and English Social networking
Listening: Students' plans for the future **Speaking:** Offering, requesting and accepting help	**Working with words:** verb + preposition phrasal verbs **Study skills:** difficult words **Pronunciation:** connected speech	**Reading:** American sci-fi **Listening:** Favourite science fiction books versus films **CLIL:** Physics and English Light and telescopes
Listening: A conversation at a forum **Speaking:** Giving and taking messages	**Working with words:** words that are easy to confuse irregular nouns **Study skills:** synonyms **Pronunciation:** words ending in /p/ and /b/, /k/ and /g/, /f/ and /v/	**Reading:** A Maori tradition **Listening:** An interview with a Maori girl **CLIL:** Social science and English Citizenship: helping others
Listening: Conversations connected with travel **Speaking:** Offering help, requesting information, making suggestions and giving instructions	**Working with words:** adjectives and adverbs verb + noun combinations **Study skills:** reading a text **Pronunciation:** difficult words	**Reading:** The Caribbean **Listening:** Someone talking about their holiday in the Caribbean **CLIL:** Geography and English Geotourism

Starter

1 S1 **Read and listen to four friends. Which of them have got the same favourite school subjects or hobbies?**

2 **Answer the questions about Lauren and Jack.**

1 How old is Lauren?
2 What did the hockey team win last year?
3 What does she want to do this year?
4 Where does Jack live?
5 What does he do at weekends?
6 When did he join a folk group?

3 **Write questions about Aneta and Lee.**

1 Where / be / Aneta / from?
2 When / she / move / to England?
3 What / she / do / on Saturdays?
4 Where / be / Lee / born?
5 What / be / his ambition?
6 What / he / do / last year?

Speaking

4 **Work in pairs. Ask and answer the questions in Exercise 3.**

“Hello. My name's Lauren. My mum is from Ireland, so I'm half-Irish. I'm 15 and I'm in Year 10. My favourite subjects are PE and biology. I love sports and I play in the school hockey team. Last year, we won the girls' hockey tournament. I like water sports too. This year, I want to join the rowing club in my town.”

“Hi. I'm Jack. I live next door to Lauren. We both enjoy playing tennis in the park at weekends. My favourite subjects at school are PE and music. I play the violin and the piano. I started the violin when I was six. Two years ago, I joined a folk group. This month we're taking part in a folk music festival.”

“My name's Aneta. I'm Polish. My family moved to England when I was seven. My hobbies are reading and acting. I love reading detective stories and thrillers, and I go to the theatre on Saturdays. I want to be a writer or maybe an actress when I leave school.”

“I'm Lee. I was born in England, but my dad's family is from China. My favourite school subjects are maths and science. My ambition is to go to university and study to be a doctor. I love street dance and last year I joined a dance group. Aneta is my best friend and I love reading too.”

Home and school

1

> Grammar

Learn about the present simple and present continuous uses of verbs, and verbs without a continuous form.

> Vocabulary

Learn words for places in homes and schools, school subjects, and adjectives to describe personality. Work with positive and negative adjectives, and *do* and *make*.

> Skills

Read about teenagers living in the UK, schools, and studying in the Australian outback.

Listen to a student talking about her school, and a teacher talking about his school.

Write a personal email.

> Communicate

Make greetings and introductions.

1 Work in pairs. Look at the photo. What kind of building do you think this is? Why?

2 1.1 Listen to three conversations (1–3). Where are the people?

3 Work in pairs. Write a list of things in your homes. Can you use every letter of the alphabet?

e.g. A – armchair, B – bath, C – cupboard ...

4 Work in pairs. Take turns to describe your home. Use the words in the vocabulary box to help you.

bathroom bedroom bungalow
dining room flat floor garage
garden hall house kitchen
living room study toilet

1A A new life

Every year, more than 26,000 children arrive in Britain. We ask some new arrivals what they like best about their new lives and what's different from home.

Home | Articles | Games | E-Cards | Glossary | Teachers | Archive | Mailbox

Daisy and Luke, the USA

My brother and I like living here in Brighton, it's cool! My brother loves the British accent: 'tomato,' and 'banana'. Everybody here is very polite too. But we don't understand all your strange words – we say 'yard' not 'garden', and 'apartment' not 'flat', you know? We have a big bungalow with a pool in the USA. Here we live in a three-storey house. Our bedrooms are on the top floor and the kitchen is on the ground floor. It seems a long way! My brother is too lazy to come downstairs for breakfast. The food is better here. There's Indian, Chinese and Thai. At home we eat too much fast food. I hate fast food. Well, OK, I don't hate it. But it's so unhealthy, you know?

Jarek, Poland

I don't know anybody from Poland here in Manchester, but I'm lucky because the English boy next door is my age. He's very friendly and kind. At home we live in a block of flats, but here we have a house. My new school is really big. I'm always late for my classes. The teachers understand – they're very patient. And they don't give much homework. I prefer English schools. At home, the teachers seem a bit strict and serious. There are a lot of rules. Here, students go out of school and buy pizza or burgers at lunchtime. We can't do that in Poland.

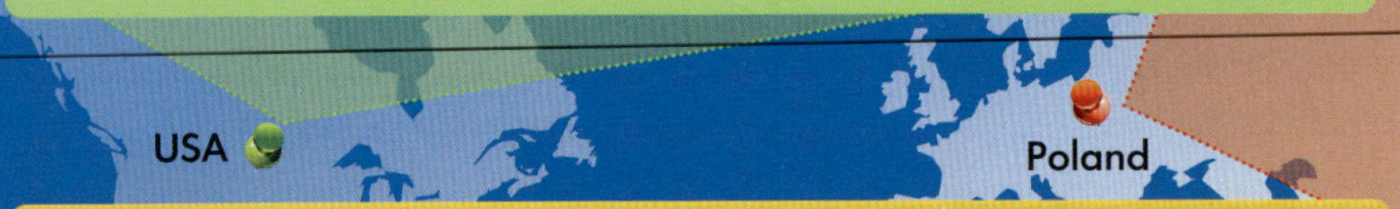

Zinah, India

It's too cold and windy here in Cambridge! I hate doing sports, especially outside in winter. The teacher at my new school is very serious about sports, but I'm not competitive. I prefer science and maths. I love the maths class because the teacher is really funny. I want to go to the Science Museum in London, but London is so big and the people seem unfriendly. We're from a small village in India. I know all the people and places. In London, I need a map!

Reading and listening

1 Read the introduction on the webpage. What do you think the new arrivals will talk about?

families food friends houses people schools teachers the weather

2 1.2 Read and listen to the webpage. Check your answers to Exercise 1.

3 Read the webpage again. Are the sentences true or false?

1 Daisy and Luke want to go home to the USA.
2 Jarek's new life is different from his life in Poland.
3 Zinah likes her maths teacher.

4 Read the webpage again. Answer the questions.

1 What does Luke love about Britain?
2 What don't Daisy and Luke understand?
3 What does Jarek like about Britain?
4 Which subjects does Zinah prefer?

Grammar: present simple and verbs without a continuous form

5 Match the examples (1–3) with the meanings (a–c).

1 We eat too much fast food.
2 I want to go to the Science Museum.
3 We live in a block of flats.

a a regular habit
b a permanent state
c a feeling or thought

See Grammar Explorer: Page 117

6 **Find these verbs in the webpage. Then use them to complete the table.**

like love understand live seem
eat prefer go out need

regular habits
buy ..... give ....
permanent states
have ....
feelings and thoughts
hate ..... know ..... want ....
....

See Grammar Explorer: Page 117

7 **Complete the sentences with the correct form of six of the verbs in the box.**

hate know like love need
prefer seem understand want

1 It's my first day. I don't .... anybody in my class.
2 London .... very big to me.
3 It's my friend's birthday soon. He .... an MP3 player.
4 My spelling is terrible. I .... a dictionary.
5 I .... Chinese food to Indian food.
6 My grandfather doesn't .... English.

8 **Work in pairs. Complete the conversations with the verbs in the box in Exercise 7. Then practise.**

1 A: Do you .... a sandwich?
B: No thanks, I'm not hungry.
2 A: Do you .... living in Britain?
B: Yes, but I .... the USA.
3 A: Can you do this maths homework?
B: No, I .... a calculator.
4 A: Our new PE teacher .... a bit serious.
B: I know!

Vocabulary: personality adjectives

9 **Choose the correct option.**

1 My friend is so **funny / friendly**. She makes us laugh a lot.
2 Our new neighbours are **lazy / kind**. They always help us.
3 My brother always wants to win. He's too **polite / competitive**.
4 There are lots of rules in our school. It's very **strict / patient**.
5 My grandfather never laughs. He's very **serious / lucky**.

Working with words: positive adjective → negative adjective

10 **Look at the examples. Then find another adjective starting with *un* in the webpage.**

My neighbour is friendly.
The people in London seem unfriendly.

See Working with words: Page 101

Speaking

11 **Write the names of people you know for each adjective in Exercise 9.**

e.g. serious – my uncle Bill

12 **Work in pairs. Tell your partner about six people from Exercise 11. Take turns.**

A: *My uncle Bill is a bit serious. He never smiles or laughs.*
B: *Well, my uncle Sam is very funny. He tells great jokes.*

Fast finishers

Which is the odd one out in each list? Why? Write more lists for a partner.

1 apartment chair flat house
2 armchair bed microwave sofa
3 bath shower sink TV
4 door kitchen roof wall

1B School life

A day at Central High School

Matt Jones

It's only my third week at my new school and I love it! Today's Friday – the best day of the week at Central High.

Why? Well, my first class on Fridays is music. I'm learning to play the trumpet this year and I love it! I practise every lunchtime in the music room because I'm not very good at the moment - I make a terrible noise!

Then we have maths. We do a test every Friday but I'm quite good at maths, so it's OK. After maths we have English. It's probably my favourite subject. I'm in the English class now – we're doing a project called 'A day at Central High School' for the school website. It's very quiet at the moment because everybody's writing their projects. I can hear the class next door. They're reading aloud from Shakespeare's Julius Caesar. Actually, that's a good play for our school because there aren't many parts in it for girls! Outside, on the sports field, the rugby team is practising for the match on Saturday. Mr Fleming, the PE teacher, is shouting at them. Our school's brilliant at rugby, actually. We often win the Schools' Cup.

Friday afternoons are great because we can choose our classes. This term I'm doing food technology. We make some fantastic dishes – spaghetti bolognese, chocolate cake, biscuits! Who says cooking is just for girls?

a

b

Speaking

1 **Put the words in the box into two groups: school subjects and places in a school. Can you add any more words to your lists?**

> art room   chemistry   dining room
> food technology   geography
> gym   hall   history   IT room
> language laboratory   library   maths
> music room   sports field   technology room

2 **Work in pairs. Describe what you're doing and let your partner guess the place. Take turns.**

A: *I'm listening to a conversation in French.*

B: *You're in the language laboratory.*

Reading and listening

3 **STUDY SKILLS Look at the photos. Find three things that are the same or different in your school.**

4 1.3 **Read and listen to the text. Which photo is Central High School? How do you know?**

5 **Read the text again. Why does Matt like Fridays? Find three reasons.**

Listening

6 1.4 **Listen to Suzi Wade, a student at an all-girls school. What does Suzi talk about?**

- **a** The places at Oaklands School.
- **b** Her favourite subjects and teachers.
- **c** The reasons all-girls schools are better.

7 1.4 **Listen again. Complete the sentences with *Girls* or *Boys*.**

1. .... are more responsible.
2. .... are better at languages.
3. .... are good at making things.

Speaking

8 **Work in pairs. Do you agree with the sentences in Exercise 7? Why? / Why not?**

Working with words: *do* and *make*

9 **Look at the examples. Then read the text quickly and find other examples of *make* and *do*.**

We're doing a project.

We're making a cake.

See Working with words: Page 101

Grammar: present simple and present continuous

10 **Find the present continuous verbs and the present simple verbs in the text.**

11 **Do we use the present simple or present continuous to describe the things below?**

1. An activity in progress at or around the time of speaking.
2. A regular or repeated activity.
3. A state or feeling.

See Grammar Explorer: Page 117

12 **Complete the sentences with the present simple or present continuous form of the verbs.**

e.g. This term in chemistry, we *are learning* about metals. (**learn**)

1. Our class usually .... gymnastics on Mondays. (**do**)
2. We .... rugby this term. (**play**)
3. 'What's that terrible noise?' 'It's John. He .... the violin.' (**practise**)
4. My friend loves reading. She .... two books every week. (**read**)
5. That's another goal! We .... by three goals to one, now. (**win**)
6. We .... a model of our school in art at the moment. (**make**)

13 **Complete the paragraph with the correct form of the verbs: present simple or present continuous.**

This year, Mark (**1**) .... (**study**) ten subjects. He (**2**) .... (**have**) about five hours of lessons every day. His best subjects (**3**) .... (**be**) technology and IT. In technology, he (**4**) .... (**make**) a robot. And in IT this term, they (**5**) .... (**learn**) about virtual reality. Mark (**6**) .... (**enjoy**) school, but he (**7**) .... (**not / like**) homework. He (**8**) .... (**get**) homework most days. He (**9**) .... (**do**) his homework in his bedroom and he (**10**) .... (**listen**) to music at the same time.

14 **Rewrite the paragraph in Exercise 13 with information about you.**

e.g. *This year, I'm studying ...*

Speaking

15 **Write questions about the information in Exercise 14. Ask your partner. Take turns.**

e.g. *How many subjects are you studying this year?*

Study skills

Using pictures

1. Before you read or listen to a text, look at the pictures.
2. Write words in English of the things you see.
3. When you read or listen, check for your ideas and words.

1C Greetings and introductions

Reading and listening

1 1.5 **Read and listen to the dialogue. Who is the man in the photo?**

2 **Find these ways of introducing and greeting people in the dialogue.**

This is …

Let me introduce …

How do you do?

Lauren:	Hi, Jack. How are you?
Jack:	I'm fine. And you?
Lauren:	I'm great! I had a fantastic time in Ireland.
Jack:	Do you want to come to the park for a game of tennis?
Lauren:	Yes, but my cousin and her parents are here at the moment. They're staying with us for a few days.
Jack:	That's OK. Your cousin can come too.
Lauren:	OK. Why don't you come in first, and meet Erin and my uncle? My aunt is out shopping with my mum, but you can meet her later.
Jack:	OK. Sure.
Lauren:	Erin. This is my friend, Jack. He lives next door.
Erin:	Hello, Jack.
Jack:	Hello, Erin. Nice to meet you.
Erin:	Nice to meet you too.
Lauren:	Let me introduce my uncle, Professor Taggart.
Jack:	How do you do, Professor?
Erin's dad:	How do you do, Jack? Call me Mr Taggart. I'm only Professor Taggart when I'm working.
Jack:	OK. Pleased to meet you, Mr Taggart.
Erin's dad:	And I'm very pleased to meet you, Jack. I hear you play a good game of tennis.
Jack:	Well … I play a lot of tennis in the summer, so I'm not bad. I'm better than Lauren, anyway!
Lauren:	I'm not sure about that! Erin's brilliant at tennis and I'm learning a lot from her. We practise every day.
Erin:	I've got an idea. Why don't I play Jack first? Then we can see who's the best!
Lauren:	Yes, let's do that.
Erin:	OK. Let's go, then. Bye, Dad.
Jack:	Goodbye, Mr. Taggart.
Lauren:	Bye, Uncle Sean. See you later!
Erin's dad:	Bye. Have a good time!

3 1.6 **Listen and repeat the *Useful expressions*. Focus on your intonation.**

USEFUL EXPRESSIONS

Informal: for greeting and introducing people your own age, or people you know well.

A: Hi, Jack. How are you?
B: I'm fine. And you?
A: I'm great!

A: This is my friend, Jack.
B: Nice to meet you, Jack.
C: Nice to meet you too.

Formal: for introducing people in a polite way.

A: Let me introduce my uncle, Professor Taggart.
B: How do you do, Professor?
C: How do you do, Jack? Call me Mr Taggart.
B: Pleased to meet you, Mr Taggart.

4 1.7 **Listen to four statements twice. Choose the best response (a, b or c).**

1 a Hello. Nice to meet you.
  b I'm fine. And you?
  c Hi.

2 a How are you?
  b I'm fine, thanks.
  c How do you do?

3 a Pleased to meet you, Mrs Smith
  b Hello, Grandma.
  c Call me Shirley.

4 a Hello, Lauren. Nice to meet you.
  b Nice to meet you, too.
  c I'm fine, thanks.

Pronunciation: stressed words and weak forms /ə/

5 1.8 **Listen to these sentences from the dialogue. Is the underlined word stressed or unstressed?**

1 Hi, Jack. How are you?
2 I had a fantastic time in Ireland.
3 Pleased to meet you, Mr Taggart.
4 How do you do, Professor?
5 Erin's brilliant at tennis.

6 1.8 **Listen to the sentences again. Words which don't give important information are not stressed and the vowel sound is weak: /ə/. Which words which have an /ə/ sound? Practise saying the sentences.**

Speaking

7 Work in groups of three. Write dialogues for each situation. Then take a role each and practise your dialogues.

1 You go to your friend's party and greet him/her. Your friend introduces you to her brother/sister.
Roles:
(**a**) you (**b**) your friend (**c**) your friend's brother/sister.

2 You're shopping with your mum/dad. You meet your new form teacher in the street. Introduce your teacher to your mum/dad.
Roles:
(**a**) you (**b**) your mum/dad (**c**) your teacher.

Writing: a personal email

1 Lee is writing an email to his brother. Read the email and answer the questions.

1 Why does Lee like his teacher?
2 Why has he got a lot of homework?
3 Why does his dance group need a good name?

2 Find *and, but, because* and *so* in the email.

See Grammar Explorer: Page 117

3 Complete the sentences with *and, but, because* or *so*.

1 I don't know many people in my class, ... they all seem very nice.
2 I meet my best friend at 8 a.m. .... we walk to school together.
3 I'm on the school team this year, ... I go to football practice every lunchtime.
4 Everybody seems more serious .... we've got exams this year.

4 Write an email to a friend or relation about your studies, your teachers and your hobbies.

To: cheng41@mailonline.uk
From: lee321@yoohu.uk
Subject: First week at school.

Hi Cheng,

How are you? How's university? I'm back at school, of course! I've got a new form teacher, Miss Jones. She's an excellent teacher, but she's really strict! She teaches science and she's brilliant at explaining new ideas. I like her because she's friendly and doesn't shout.

We've got a lot of exams this year, so I have to do homework every night. I also practise with my dance group four times a week. We're practising really hard at the moment because we've got an audition for a big talent competition. We need a cool name for our group. Have you got any ideas?

Mum's calling me for dinner, so I must go now. I think we're having chicken with chips! My favourite!

Love,
Lee

1D Education in the outback

Reading

1 **Look at the photos. What can you see? What do you know about the Australian outback?**

2 1.9 **Read the article. Can you explain the title?**

3 **Read the text again and answer the questions.**

1. Where do children in the outback live?
2. How do they study?
3. When do students meet?
4. How are outback students different?

4 **Find words in the text that mean the same as the underlined words.**

1. Some of the farms are for cows.
2. Outback children don't go to normal schools.
3. Students connect online to their classes.
4. Every week there's a meeting of the whole school.

Culture

Australia online: the world's largest classroom

The Australian outback is one of the most isolated parts of the world. It covers a huge area of more than 1.5 million square kilometres. The towns are hundreds of kilometres apart. Most people live on sheep farms or cattle stations. Outback children are different to children from urban areas. They study at home and don't attend traditional schools. Many of them work on the family farm from an early age. They learn to ride horses and to survive in difficult situations. This means that they are more mature and better at studying alone than city children. They are also good at organising their work.

Young outback children study with the School of the Air, and older students can enrol at a School Of Distance Education (SODE). About 15 percent of the students are Aborigines. In the past, students and teachers used two-way radio. The name 'School of the Air' comes from that time. Today, teachers give lessons by satellite and use an electronic whiteboard. Most students have a satellite dish and a computer with a webcam. They log in to classes in real time and can see their teacher on their computer screen. The teacher can demonstrate skills in science, music, art, PE, drama or poetry. Students can also talk to each other and to the teacher.

As well as attending classes, students also have to do coursework and exams, and younger children have an online school assembly once a week. In addition, there are opportunities for students to meet. Three or four times a year, students travel to the nearest centre to take part in different activities, such as sports week and school excursions.

Listening

5 1.10 **Listen to a teacher from an Australian School of Distance Education (SODE). Are the sentences true or false?**

1 Michael Sheen teaches science.
2 He teaches very young children.
3 He does experiments in front of a large class.
4 The students don't listen to his lessons.
5 Many students don't do their coursework.
6 Students often get better results than students at an ordinary school.

6 1.10 **Michael Sheen talks about the similarities and differences between teaching in a regular school and teaching at a SODE. Listen and complete the sentences.**

Similarities
1 There's a lot of ....
2 We prepare our ....

Differences
3 The classroom is ....
4 He can't see the ....

Technology and English

Languages and the Internet

1 **Work in pairs. Discuss these questions with your partner.**

1 How do people use computers to communicate with each other?
2 Which languages do most people use?

2 **Read the article and check your answers.**

Modern technology helps people to stay in touch. In the past, people wrote letters or sent telegrams, and long distance telephone calls were very expensive. Today, people use computers to communicate with friends or family who live far away. Almost everybody uses email these days and internet phone connections, such as Skype, are becoming more popular every day. Young people, in particular, enjoy using webcams and social networking sites, like Facebook.

There are one billion internet users in the world today and about one third log on in English. That's because web technology started in the United States and most web pages are in English. In addition, over sixty percent of people in the UK, the US, Canada and Australia are online. However, more and more Chinese people connect to the Internet every day. Today there are more than 160 million people logging on in Chinese and experts predict that the number of users will continue to increase. Other internet languages that are growing rapidly are Spanish and Arabic.

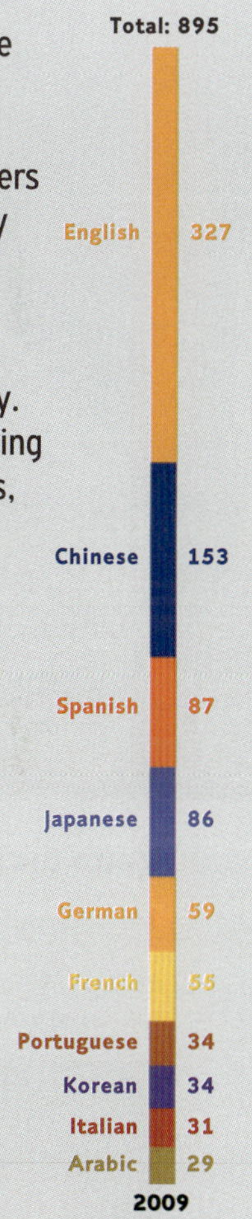

Top ten languages used on the Internet by number of users (millions)

3 **Why do you think that the number of Chinese, Spanish and Arabic internet users is growing quickly?**

Project

Write about your school. Describe the buildings, the classrooms, subjects, other activities, etc. What are the students and teachers good at? Include some photos.

TRUE STORY

A different kind of explorer

Benedict Allen Explores Life

Benedict Allen lives a life filled with excitement and danger. He crosses deserts, mountains and rivers to find the kind of people and places we can only dream about.

But Allen is not like most explorers. He always tries to travel without modern technology like telephones. And he doesn't take a team to film him – just a camera. So, when he is travelling, very often no one knows where he is! He says this is good because he lives the same kind of life as the people he visits. He wants to get close to native people and explore how they live.

So why does he do it? He says he goes on his journeys to try to understand the world and to discover different ways of seeing it. Then he writes books about his travels so we can follow his adventures and discoveries. And what is his favourite place? For Benedict Allen that's an easy question to answer – the Namib Desert. He says it's like paradise!

1 Match the items (1–6) to the pictures (a–f).

1 map and compass
2 camel
3 canoe
4 desert
5 coast
6 volcano

a ....

b ....

c ....

d ....

e ....

f ....

2 Read the text and complete the sentences using the correct form of the verbs in the box.

try	live	get	write	cross	travel

1 Benedict Allen .... an exciting and dangerous life.
2 He .... deserts, rivers and mountains.
3 He .... without things like telephones.
4 He .... very close to native people.
5 He .... to understand the world and find other ways of seeing it.
6 He .... books about his travels.

3 Imagine you are an explorer. In pairs, take turns telling each other something you do, and asking questions.

e.g. A: *I travel without a mobile phone. Do you?*
B: *No, I don't. I always keep my mobile phone with me.*

Do you ... meet interesting people? / cross mountains? / travel with camels? / take a laptop? / etc.

NATIONAL GEOGRAPHIC

Performers & Artists 2

> Grammar

Learn about *there was / there were*, the past simple, the past continuous and the present perfect.

> Vocabulary

Learn words for music, musicians, and adjectives to describe music.

Work with adjectives, nouns, and verbs.

> Skills

Read about the history of hip-hop, musical lives, and artists' lives and work.

Listen to a biography of a musician, and people's opinions of an artist's work.

Write a diary.

> Communicate

Ask for information on the phone.

1 **Work in pairs. Look at the photo. What kinds of music can you play on this instrument?**

2 2.1 **Listen to six music clips (1–6). What musical styles are they? Use the words in the vocabulary box to help you.**

blues	classical	country	dance	
folk	gospel	hip-hop	jazz	jungle
opera	pop	reggae	rock	soul

3 **Work in pairs. Which musical styles are popular in your country?**

4 **Answer the questions. Then ask your partner. What have you got in common?**

1. What kinds of music do you listen to?
2. Who are your favourite performers?
3. Did you go to any concerts last year? Which ones?
4. Do you play any instruments? Which ones?

2A Hip-hop planet

Hip-hop planet

By James McBride, jazz musician and author.

You can find hip-hop everywhere you go. Countries like France, Brazil and even Japan have their own hip-hop culture. But where did this strange speaking – singing style come from? Many centuries ago, in West Africa, traditional storytellers played musical instruments while they were telling stories. When this tradition travelled from West Africa to the USA, it developed into different musical styles. For example, blues, jazz and soul music. These styles all started in poor, African-American areas. And in the 1970s, there were a lot of poor areas in New York. There wasn't any money for music lessons in schools, so kids made their own music. Teenagers Afrika Bambaataa and Kool DJ Herc played their records outside in the streets. Everybody joined in. MCs had rapping competitions. Every week, there were talented new dancers, new DJs and new MCs. Hip-hop culture was born.

I remember the first time I heard hip-hop. It was 1980. I was at a party in New York. There was a young DJ at the party. He was playing records on two turntables. While he was putting a record on, a kid picked up a microphone and began rapping. Some other kids were break-dancing to the music. It was loud and repetitive, and I hated it. I preferred jazz.

During the 1980s, hip-hop became popular all over the USA. Today's successful artists like Missy Elliot and her friend Tim Mosley (Timbaland) heard it on the radio when they were growing up.

The last time I heard hip-hop, I was in Senegal, West Africa. I was writing a book about African-Americans. I was going to interview a traditional storyteller when I met a young hip-hop artist. He told me there are hundreds of rap groups in Africa today. We live on a hip-hop planet.

Reading and listening

1 Work in pairs. How much do you know about hip-hop? Compare your answers with another pair.

Hip-hop trivia:

which is the correct answer?

1 Hip-hop artists wear **a)** hippy clothes **b)** jewellery.
2 The DJ plays **a)** records **b)** CDs.
3 The DJ uses **a)** an MP3 player **b)** turntables.
4 The singer is called **a)** the MC **b)** the crew.
5 The dancers are called **a)** rappers **b)** break-dancers.

2 2.2 **Read and listen to the text. What is the article about?**

a Hip-hop culture in Africa and Europe.
b The most famous hip-hop artists today.
c The history of hip-hop music.

3 Read the text again. Are the sentences true or false? Correct the false information.

1 Traditional storytelling styles came to America from Africa.
2 Hip-hop began in Senegal.
3 The first rappers were Missy Elliot and Timbaland.
4 James McBride was a DJ.

Working with words: nouns → adjectives

4 Look at the examples. Then find another similar adjective in the text.

tradition: I was looking for a tradition**al** storyteller.
talent: there were talent**ed** new dancers.

See Working with words: Page 102

Grammar: *there was / there were*

5 Complete the sentences from the text.

1 There .... a young DJ at the party.
2 There .... a lot of poor areas in New York.
3 There .... any money for music lessons.

See Grammar Explorer: Page 117

6 Read the first sentence. Complete the second sentence so that it gives the same information.

1 **a** A lot of people were at the party.
b There .... a lot of people at the party.

2 **a** CDs didn't exist in the 1970s.
b There .... any CDs in the 1970s.

3 **a** The band didn't have a singer.
b There .... no singer with the band.

4 **a** The radio played some great music.
b There .... some great music on the radio.

Grammar: past simple and past continuous

7 Find the past simple verbs and the past continuous verbs in the text.

8 Do we use the past simple or past continuous to describe the things below?

1 An activity in progress at a specific time.
2 A completed action at a specific time.
3 A sequence of completed actions.

See Grammar Explorer: Page 118

9 Complete the sentences from the text with *when*, *while* or *during*.

1 .... this tradition travelled from West Africa to the USA, it developed into different musical styles.
2 .... he was putting a record on, a kid picked up a microphone and began rapping.
3 .... the 1980s, hip-hop became popular all over the USA.
4 I was going to interview a traditional storyteller .... I met a young hip-hop artist.

See Grammar Explorer: Page 118

10 Complete the text with the past simple or past continuous form of the verbs.

Missy Elliot and Tim Mosley (**1**) grew up (**grow up**) in the same town. Missy Elliot (**2**) .... (**start**) her band, Sista, in 1990. She (**3**) .... (**sing**) with her band when a New York record producer (**4**) .... (**hear**) her. She (**5**) .... (**move**) to New York. Tim Mosley (**6**) .... (**go**) with her and he (**7**) .... (**change**) his name to Timbaland. While she (**8**) .... (**live**) in New York, Missy Elliot (**9**) .... (**write**) songs for other hip-hop artists. Timbaland and Missy Elliot both (**10**) .... (**become**) international stars in the 1990s.

Speaking

11 Match the comments (1–4) with the pictures (a–d).

1 'I think it's sad.'
2 'I can't stand it. It's too loud and aggressive.'
3 'I like it. It's catchy.'
4 'I don't mind it. But it's a bit boring.'

12 Work in pairs. What do you think of the different styles of music on page 15? Ask and answer questions using the adjectives in the box below.

e.g. A: *I think classical music is really relaxing. Do you like it?*
B: *No. I think it's boring.*

aggressive awful boring catchy exciting great happy loud relaxing repetitive romantic sad strange

Fast finishers

How many adjectives do you know to describe these things? Write at least five adjectives for each thing. Then write adjectives with the opposite meaning.

performers sports people places you go food

2B Musicians

MUSICAL LIVES

What does it feel like to give a concert performance at the age of seven? Or to be world-famous when you are ten? These were the experiences of Chopin, Michael Jackson and many other child prodigies. Did they lead normal lives when they were growing up? Or did they spend all of their time practising the piano or rehearsing dance moves? What about some of today's talented young musicians?

Simone Porter was born in 1997 and she began playing the violin when she was three. Simone has performed with orchestras around the world and in 2008 she appeared in front of an audience of over 40,000 people. Simone is artistic as well as musical. In her free time she likes writing and drawing. In fact, she's designed all her concert dresses.

Michael Province is another successful young violinist. Michael has won first place in many classical music competitions and appeared on TV. Michael spends a lot of time practising. He's got a lot of friends but he hasn't got enough time for them or for a social life.

Composer, conductor and pianist Alex is in a similar situation. Music has dominated his life. He's only 16, but he's written over 40 pieces of music. When he was attending a London school, he had a difficult time with bullies. He had lessons at home for a year and then entered the St Petersburg Conservatory.

These three young people haven't had 'normal' childhoods. Have their lives been better or worse than ordinary kids'? What do you think?

1 **Look at the words for musicians. Which ones play instruments? Which instruments do they play?**

artist cellist composer conductor
drummer guitarist harpist
keyboard player pianist singer
trumpeter violinist

2 **Work in pairs. Compare your answers to Exercise 1. How many more instruments can you name?**

3 **What instruments do these musicians play? Add four more names then test your partner.**

Nelly Furtado Alicia Keys Justin Timberlake

Working with words: nouns and verbs → nouns

4 **Look at the examples. Which nouns in the in Exercise 1 have a similar form?**

guitar: I want to be a guitarist.

trumpet: My uncle is a trumpeter.

See Working with words: Page 102

Reading and listening

5 STUDY SKILLS **Read the text quickly. How many words for musicians and instruments can you find?**

6 2.3 **Read and listen to the text. Find the names of five people. What have they got in common?**

7 **Read the text again. Complete the sentences with the correct names.**

1 .... doesn't go to ordinary school.
2 .... has other interests as well as music.
3 .... doesn't see friends very often.
4 .... writes and performs music.

Speaking

8 **Work in groups of four. Read the last paragraph of the text again. Give your opinions.**

Grammar: present perfect

9 Complete the sentences from the text.

1. Simone .... with orchestras around the world.
2. These three young people .... 'normal' childhoods.
3. .... their lives .... better or worse than ordinary kids?

Note that the present perfect form – the past participle – of some verbs is irregular.

10 Find seven more present perfect verbs in the text. Then choose the correct option.

We use the present perfect when we **give /don't give** the date of the event.

See Grammar Explorer: Page 118

11 Complete the text with the present perfect form of the verbs.

Goldie is a British DJ and graffiti artist. He (**1**) has recorded (**record**) many drum and bass CDs and he (**2**) .... (**have**) exhibitions of his paintings. Goldie (**3**) .... (**be**) in a James Bond film and he (**4**) .... (**take part**) in a competition for conductors on TV. He (**5**) .... (**not / have**) any formal music lessons. He (**6**) .... (**write**) a classical music piece for the BBC, but he (**7**) .... (**not / learn**) how to read music.

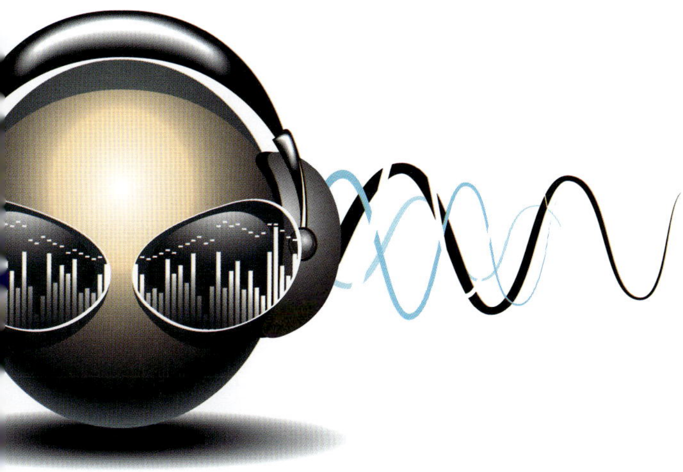

Listening

12 2.4 **Listen to the biography of the violinist Vanessa-Mae. Which words from the box do you hear?**

London	talent	performed	pop
techno	classical	awards	festival

13 2.4 **Listen again and complete the notes.**

1. Vanessa-Mae was born in ....
2. She plays the .... and the ....
3. She recorded Beethoven and Tchaikovsky when she was ....
4. She has recorded with .... and ....
5. She has sold more than .... albums.

Speaking

14 Work in pairs. Do you think Vanessa-Mae is unusual? Why? / Why not?

15 Make notes about a musician or singer. Then work in pairs. Take turns to describe the person, and to ask and answer questions. Can you guess your partner's person?

A: *... and he's also won a lot of MTV awards.*

B: *Has he been in any films?*

Study skills

Topic words

1. With a new text, look and listen for words that are connected to the same topic.
2. Learn the words by writing them in groups: **e.g.** *orchestral instruments – violin, piano, ...*
3. Use your own categories to organise words: **e.g.** *music I like: jazz, hip-hop, techno, ...*

2C Asking for information

Reading and listening

1 2.5 **Read and listen to the dialogue. What does Lee ask for information about?**

- **a** pop concerts
- **b** music shows
- **c** art exhibitions

Saleswoman:	Hello, West End Box Office. How can I help you?
Lee:	Hello. I'm phoning about tickets for this Saturday.
Saleswoman:	Which show would you like to see?
Lee:	Have you got tickets for *Abba, the Musical*?
Saleswoman:	Sorry. There aren't any tickets left for *Abba*.
Lee:	What about *Les Miserables*? Or *Stomp*?
Saleswoman:	I'm afraid we've only got tickets for the afternoon performance of *Stomp*.
Lee:	Oh, right. What time does the show start?
Saleswoman:	It starts at four o'clock.
Lee:	OK. How much do the tickets cost?
Saleswoman:	They're fifty pounds each.
Lee:	Fifty pounds! Can you hold on a moment, please?
Aneta:	That's OK for me. My mum's buying the ticket for my birthday.
Lee:	Yes, but what about Lauren and Jack?
Aneta:	We can phone them and ask.
Lee:	Hello? Sorry to keep you waiting. Can I phone back later?
Saleswoman:	Yes, of course.
Lee:	Great. Thanks for your help.
Saleswoman:	You're welcome. Goodbye.
Lee:	Goodbye.

2 Read the dialogue again. Why doesn't Lee buy any tickets?

- **a** There aren't any tickets left.
- **b** He hasn't got any money.
- **c** He wants to talk to Lauren and Jack first.

3 **Read the dialogue again. Put the *Useful expressions* in the correct order (1–10). Who says them - Lee or the saleswoman.**

USEFUL EXPRESSIONS

... I'm phoning about (tickets for this Saturday).
... Sorry. There aren't any tickets left (for *Abba*).
... How much do (the tickets) cost?
... You're welcome.
... How can I help you?
... Can you hold on a moment, please?
... What time does (the show start)?
... Can I phone back later?
... Thanks for your help.
... I'm afraid we've only got tickets for (the afternoon performance of *Stomp*).

4 2.6 **Listen and repeat the *Useful expressions*. Focus on your intonation.**

5 2.7 **Listen to the conversation and complete the information.**

Time: ....
Day: ....
Price: ....

Speaking

6 **Work in pairs. Take turns asking for and giving information about these events.**

BIG ROCK Music Festival	Live Comedy Show	Missy Elliot *Live!*
Sat & Sun, 11 a.m. 'til midnight Riverside Park	Every Friday & Saturday 9 p.m. .... Roundhouse Theatre	4th–8th October 10 p.m. City Concert Hall
Tickets £25	*Tickets: £15*	**Tickets: £45**

Student A: Decide which event you want to go to. Phone the box office for information about days, times and prices.

Student B: You work in the box office. You don't have many tickets left. For each event, choose only one day when there are tickets left.

Pronunciation: the sounds /t/ and /d/ before /j/

7 2.8 **Listen to the dialogue. Which sound joins the underlined words? Choose /tʃ/ or /dʒ/.**

A: Have you got your ticket yet? /tʃ/ /dʒ/
B: Yes, it arrived yesterday. /tʃ/ /dʒ/

8 2.9 **Listen and repeat the sentences.**

1 When did you last go to a concert?
2 Vanessa-Mae sold millions of albums last year.
3 I like classical music, but you don't.
4 The music festival ended yesterday.

Writing: a diary

1 **Read Aneta's diary entry. Answer the questions.**

1 Where did Aneta go?
2 Who did she go with?
3 Which places did she visit?
4 What were her opinions?
5 What did she do after the show?

2 **Find the following linking words in the text: *first, then, after, after that, before, during* and *in the end.***

See Grammar Explorer: Page 119

3 **Choose the correct option or options.**

I went shopping today. (**1**) First, / During / Before I bought some clothes. (**2**) After / After that, / Then, I had lunch in a burger bar. I wanted a cheeseburger or a salad, but they were sold out. (**3**) Before / First, / In the end, I had a sandwich. (**4**) After that, / Before / After lunch, I went to the bookshop. (**5**) Then, / After that, / During I caught the bus home.

4 **Write a diary entry about a day in your recent past. Use the questions in Exercise 1 to help you plan your paragraph.**

Saturday, 10 October

I had a great time in London today! I got up really early and met Lauren, Jack and Lee at the station. Before we left the house, my dad gave me £50 spending money! We caught the train to London and arrived at ten o'clock. First, we visited the modern art museum. The art was strange, but some of it was amazing! Then, we looked round the museum shop. After that, we were really hungry so we bought some sandwiches and ate them in the park.

In the afternoon we went to the theatre to see Stomp! It was absolutely fantastic. During the show, the audience joined in with the rhythms. After the show, we were thirsty and wanted to have a drink in the theatre bar. It was too busy, so we went to a café across the road, but there were no tables available. In the end, we bought some cans of Coke from a machine and then caught the train back home.

2D British artists

Culture

Reading

1 Work in pairs. Look at the photos of works of art. What is your opinion of them?

2 2.10 Read the text and match the photos (a–c) with the artists (1–3).

In the 1990s, several British artists became famous for their strange, new approach to painting and sculpture. But is it art?

1 **Antony Gormley** is a sculptor. He makes sculptures of the human body. His first important work was *Field*. This was a collection of 40,000 small figures. Many people helped him to make the sculptures. His most famous sculpture is *The Angel of the North*, a dramatic piece which stands on a hill in the north of England. Gormley worked on this sculpture for three years, from 1995 to 1998. In 2009, Gormley invited people to stand on a platform in Trafalgar Square, London. Each person had one hour to do what they liked. A great idea, but is it art?

2 **Banksy** began as a graffiti artist. He painted on walls and buildings, in cities all over the world. Of course, painting in the street is a crime, so Banksy decided to keep his identity a secret. When Banksy's funny, interesting street art became famous, he started showing his work in galleries and museums. In June 2009, the Banksy UK Summer Show opened in Bristol, England and included more than 100 works of art.

3 **Damian Hirst** first became famous for his artwork involving animals. His enormous pieces of work are strange and shocking. In 1990, he put a dead cow's head inside a glass case. In 1991, his exhibition included a dead shark. Hirst is also famous for his large paintings of spots and spirals. In 2007, Hirst sold a human skull covered in diamonds for 50 million pounds and became the world's richest living artist.

a

b

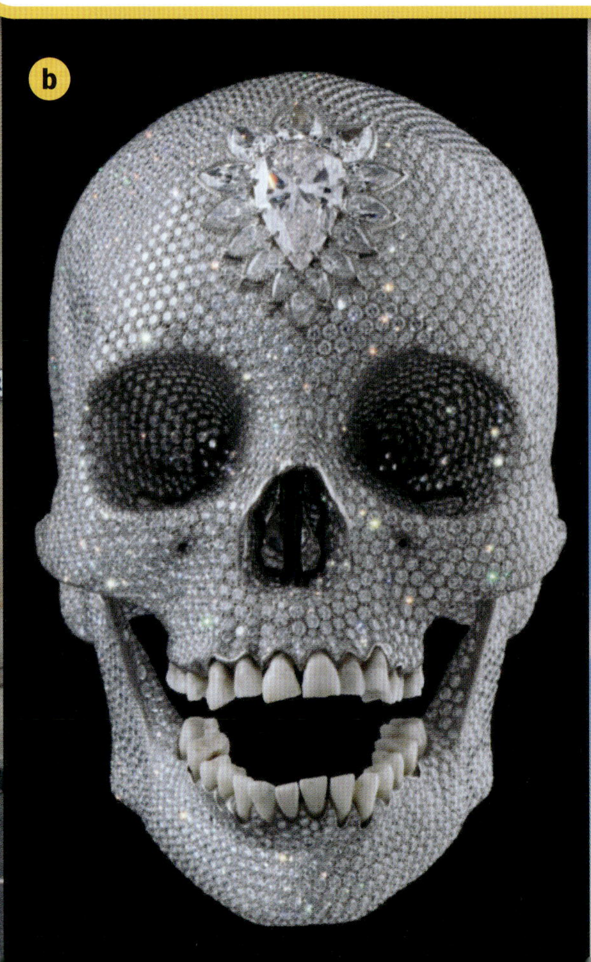

c

3 **Read the text again. Complete the sentences with the names of the artists: *Banksy*, *Hirst* or *Gormley*.**

1 ....'s real name is a mystery.
2 .... used dead animals in his exhibitions.
3 You don't need to go to a gallery to see work by .... and ....
4 .... makes sculptures of people.
5 ....'s art is very expensive.

4 **Find words in the text for these things.**

1 Places to see art.
2 Types of artwork.
3 Adjectives to describe art.

Listening

5 2.11 **Listen to three people's opinions of one of the artists. Which artist are they talking about?**

6 2.11 **Listen again. Match the number of the speaker (1, 2 or 3) to each of the summarising sentences (a-e).**

a I don't mind his work. It's quite good.
b I think some people know who he is.
c He's not an artist at all!
d I think his work is interesting and important.
e He's a very rich man.

Art and English

Vincent Van Gogh

The Red Vineyard

1 **How much do you know about Vincent Van Gogh and his work? Answer the questions.**

1 What are Van Gogh's most famous paintings?
2 Why didn't people buy his art when he was alive?
3 What happened to his ear?

2 **Read the text and check your answers**

Vincent Van Gogh

(1853–1890)

Vincent Van Gogh was born in Holland in 1853. He started painting when he was 27 years old. He started classes at famous art schools, but he didn't get on with his teachers and didn't stay long. In 1886, he lived with his brother, Theo, in Paris and painted scenes of the city. In 1888, he moved to the south of France, where he painted many of his most famous pictures, including *Vase with 12 Sunflowers* and *The Starry Night*.

During his life, Van Gogh had periods of extreme depression. At other times, he was happy and optimistic and produced hundreds of paintings. In 1890, in a clinic in France, Van Gogh shot himself. He died two days later.

Van Gogh's style of painting was new and controversial, and nobody wanted to buy his work. During his life, Van Gogh only sold one painting; *The Red Vineyard*, painted in 1888.

Van Gogh's Ear

In 1888, the artist, Paul Gauguin, was staying with Van Gogh. They were close friends, but one day they had a terrible argument. Many historians believe that Gauguin left after the fight, and that Van Gogh became very depressed and cut off part of his left ear. However, recent evidence suggests that Gauguin cut off Van Gogh's ear during the fight.

Project

Write about your favourite artist or performer. Write about their life and give your opinion of their work.

Consolidation Units 1 and 2

Reading

Identifying the main idea

- Read the whole text quickly. Don't try to understand every word. Decide what you think the main topic of the text is.
- Read the text again and look for words that are connected to that topic. This helps you check your decision.
- Look at the options in the question. Which one matches your decision the best?
- Read the text again. Check the alternative options and make sure.

Important! You need to read the whole text to find the main idea.

1 Read the text quickly. What do you think the main topic of the text is?

Last year, my family moved from London to Edinburgh. I didn't want to go, but my mum got a new job. I hated my new school at first, but I made lots of new friends and now I like it. When I started going to the new school, it was difficult to understand the Scottish accent of my new teachers. Now, when I phone my grandparents in London, they say I'm starting to get a Scottish accent!

2 Which option (a–c) best matches your answer to Exercise 1?

a Living in Scotland.
b Moving to a new place.
c Living with my family.

3 Read the text and choose the correct option (a–c).

I started to be interested in music when I was about ten years old. I was learning the piano at school and I enjoyed the lessons very much. Then I went to music classes with a private teacher. I learnt the violin and the trumpet, but I was best at the piano. While I was practising one day, I realised that I enjoyed making up my songs more than playing other people's music. I was about twelve years old. I often wrote music during my lessons at school because I wasn't interested in any other subjects!

What is the text about?

a The writer's ambitions as a musician.
b The writer's experiences of music as a student.
c The writer's experience as a professional musician.

Listening

Identifying detailed information

- Read the questions carefully before you listen. Try to predict the information you will hear.
- For gap-fill questions, decide what type of information goes into the gap.
- For true or false statements, underline the key words in the statements.

Important! Answer the questions the first time you hear the text. Check your answers if you can listen for a second time.

1 Look at the form. Then match the information (a–d) with the gaps (1–4).

The Prince's Theatre	
Booking form	
Day:	(1) ....
Performance:	(2) ....
Number of tickets:	(3) ....
Name:	(4) ....

a Richardson.
b Saturday.
c Afternoon.
d Six.

2 2.12 **Listen and check your answers.**

3 Now look at this task. What type of information is missing in each gap? Choose the correct option (a or b).

Listen to the information about a singer and complete the information.

1 She was born in ....
  a a name
  b a date

2 She sings with ....
  a a place
  b the name of a band

3 She plays ....
  a an instrument
  b a number

4 Her band has sold .... albums.
  a a place
  b a number

4 2.13 **Listen and check your answers.**

Comparing with adjectives

1 Look at the pictures and complete the sentences.

Ben's school Dan's school

1 Dan's school is .... than Ben's school. (**big**)
2 Dan's school is .... than Ben's school. (**noisy**)
3 Ben's school is .... than Dan's school. (**traditional**)
4 Ben's school is .... than Dan's school. (**modern**)
5 Dan's school is .... than Ben's school. (**good**)

We can use *isn't as* + adjective + *as* instead of *less*+ adjective + *than*.

2 Look at the example. Then complete the sentences.

Ben's school isn't as big as Dan's school.

1 Ben's school .... Dan's school. (**noisy**)
2 Ben's school .... Dan's school. (**modern**)
3 Dan's school .... Ben's school. (**traditional**)
4 Ben's school .... Dan's school. (**good**)

3 Read the first sentence. Then complete the second sentence so that it gives the same information.

1 My teachers are more serious than Ben's teachers.
Ben's teachers ....
2 My teachers aren't as friendly as Ben's teachers.
Ben's teachers ....
3 Ben's school is older than my school.
My school is ....
4 Ben's teachers are less strict than my teachers.
My teachers ....

4 Which two sentences mean the same thing?

a My school is the same as Ben's school.
b My school isn't the same as Ben's school.
c My school is different to Ben's school.

Comparing with nouns

We can also compare quantities of things with *there is / are*, + *as much / many*.

5 Look at the example. Then complete the sentences with *as much* or *as many*.

In Ben's school, there aren't as many students as in Dan's school.

1 In Ben's school, there aren't .... teachers .... in Dan's school.
2 In Ben's school, there aren't .... rules .... in Dan's school.
3 In Ben's school, there isn't .... discipline .... in Dan's school.
4 In Ben's school, they don't give .... homework .... in Dan's school.

6 Look at the example. Then rewrite the sentences in Exercise 5.

In Dan's school, there are more students than in Ben's school.

1 In Dan's school, ...
2 In Dan's school, ...
3 In Dan's school, ...
4 In Dan's school, ...

7 Complete the sentences with *as*, *than*, or *from*.

1 London is different .... my town.
2 My house is the same .... your house.
3 Rap is more boring .... reggae.
4 Hip-hop isn't as relaxing .... classical music.
5 There aren't as many rappers in the UK .... in the USA.
6 I don't listen to as much music .... my brother.
7 Pop songs are catchier .... soul music.
8 Guitar music is different .... violin music.

Review Units 1 and 2

Vocabulary

1 Write the places.

1 You sleep here. b............
2 You do experiments here. l............
3 You cook food here. k............
4 Flowers grow here. g............
5 You eat school lunch here. c............

1 mark per item: .../5 marks

2 Write the school subjects.

1 physics, biology and c............ = science
2 French and Italian = l............
3 p............ and drawing = art
4 cooking = f............ t............
5 geography and h............ = social sciences

1 mark per item: .../5 marks

3 Complete the sentences with adjectives.

1 My sister does nothing. She's l............ .
2 My parents are s .... They have lots of rules.
3 We laugh a lot in maths because the teacher is f............ .
4 Everyone is singing that song. It's very c ....
5 This music is s............ . It makes me cry.

1 mark per item: .../5 marks

4 Write the instruments.

1 ....
2 ....
3 ....
4 ....
5 ....

1 mark per item: .../5 marks

5 Complete the sentences.

1 I never like waiting. I'm ....
2 I .... a mistake in my test yesterday.
3 We .... English on Fridays.
4 Everybody knows this painter. She's very ....
5 My friend won first place in a ....

1 mark per item: .../5 marks

Grammar

6 Complete the sentences with the present simple or present continuous of these verbs.

live need play prefer want

1 I .... pop to jazz.
2 .... you .... some pasta?
3 I .... a calculator to do this maths.
4 Where's Jack? He .... rugby.
5 My best friend .... next door to me.

1 mark per item: .../5 marks

7 Complete the paragraph with the present simple or present continuous of the verbs.

I (**1**)............ (**learn**) the electric guitar this year. My cousin (**2**) .... (**teach**) me. I (**3**) .... (**practise**) in the evenings. My parents (**4**) .... (**watch**) TV. They (**5**) .... (**not / like**) the noise I make!

1 mark per item: .../5 marks

8 Write affirmative or negative sentences and questions with *there was / there were*.

1 .... a lot of people in the audience.
2 .... a concert last night?
3 .... any tickets for the show.
4 .... any rap artists in the 1970s?
5 .... a great programme on TV last night.

1 mark per item: .../5 marks

9 Complete the paragraph with the past simple or past continuous of the verbs.

Last week, my friend and I (**1**) .... (**go**) to a fantastic concert. After the show, while we (**2**) .... (**leave**) the theatre, we (**3**) .... (**see**) the singer. We (**4**) .... (**take**) his photo while he (**5**) .... (**get into**) his car.

1 mark per item: .../5 marks

10 Complete the sentences.

1 Are you good .... maths?
2 I fell asleep .... the film.
3 Geography is easier .... physics.
4 Goldie was 21 .... he made his first CD.
5 Rock isn't as interesting .... jazz.

1 mark per item: .../5 marks

Communicate

11 Complete the dialogue with the expressions.

You're welcome.
How can I help you?
How much do they cost?
Thanks for your help.
I'm phoning about

Salesman: Hello. City Hall. (**1**) ....
Aneta: (**2**) .... tickets for *Chicago*.
Salesman: Yes?
Aneta: (**3**)............. .
Salesman: We've got some tickets for Friday at £25.
Aneta: That's great. (**4**) ....
Saleswoman: (**5**) ....

2 marks per item: .../10 marks

12 Is the underlined word stressed or unstressed?

1 Jack's brilliant <u>at</u> maths.
2 We had a good time in <u>London</u>.
3 Pleased <u>to</u> meet you.
4 How do you <u>do</u>?
5 Do you want a game <u>of</u> tennis?

2 marks per item: .../10 marks

13 Match the statements (1–5) with the responses (a–e).

1 Hi, Ben. How are you?
2 How do you do, Mr Brown?
3 Let me introduce my teacher, Mrs Short.
4 See you later.
5 This is my friend, Ben.

a How do you do, Emma? Call me Bryan.
b I'm fine. And you?
c Nice to meet you, Ben.
d OK, bye.
e Pleased to meet you.

2 marks per item: .../10 marks

14 Complete the sentences with these words. Use one word twice.

and because but so

1 My maths teacher is strict .... he isn't serious.
2 On Saturday mornings I meet my friends .... we go shopping.
3 We lost the match, ... everyone's unhappy.
4 We didn't buy tickets .... they were too expensive.
5 I studied a lot, ... I didn't pass my exam.

2 marks per item: .../10 marks

15 Complete the story with these words.

after any because first for
in the end next so then while

I spent a lot of time in town yesterday! (**1**) .... , I met Emma and we did some shopping. Emma wanted to buy some jeans, (**2**) .... we went to a clothes shop. (**3**) .... we were paying for the jeans, we saw Amy. She was waiting for Ben. We talked to Amy for a few minutes. (**4**) .... we all went for something to eat. While were eating, Ben arrived. I gave him some of my pasta (**5**) .... I wasn't very hungry. (**6**)............. lunch, we went shopping again! Ben wanted to buy a Celine Dion CD (**7**) .... his mum. It's her birthday (**8**) .... week. We tried all the shops, but there weren't (**9**) .... Celine Dion CDs! (**10**) ...., he bought a scarf.

1 mark per item: .../10 marks

Total: .../100

I can...

I can make informal greetings and introductions.
I can make formal greetings and introductions.
I can ask for information on the phone.

PROJECT School timetable

	Monday
8 - 10 am	**Technology** Information Technology (IT) – Using the Internet In this lesson, students learn how to surf the web safely and effectively. There will also be information about using different search engines. Finally, this lesson teaches students about the best websites to use to continue their education online.
10 - 12 pm	**ARTS**
10.00 am	**Drama** Students learn the short section from the play that the teacher gave the previous week. During this lesson students will have the chance to act out roles with other students.
11.00 am	**Painting with watercolours** For most of this term students learn how to use watercolours properly. If the weather is good, the lesson may take place outdoors.
	LUNCH
1 - 2 pm	**Sciences** Biology or chemistry Students can choose which class to attend. In biology this week, the subject is *The Skeleton* and students will learn all about the bones in human and animal skeletons. Alternatively, students can study chemistry. This class takes place in the science laboratory, and the subject of the lesson this week is *How explosions happen*.
2 - 4 pm	**SPORTS**
2 pm	**Theory** Students learn about the tactics involved in a certain sport. We use video equipment to see real action from past games.
3 pm	**Practice** After we have picked teams, students will play a short match lasting 45 minutes. This week, the sports are rugby (for boys) and hockey (for girls).
	Homework IT – the teacher will give students websites to look up at home (about 30 minutes) Drama – students have to learn a part for the next lesson. (30-60 minutes) Biology/chemistry – students have to write a short report of the lesson (about 20 minutes)

1 Read the school timetable. Are the sentences true or false?

1. There is no homework today for chemistry. **T / F**
2. You need to be prepared for your ten o'clock lesson today. **T / F**
3. You may watch a football match today. **T / F**
4. Students have to do both biology and chemistry today. **T / F**
5. The first lesson of the day is about computers. **T / F**
6. There are two lessons today where you might go outside. **T / F**

2 Match the school subjects in the box to their categories. Add any other subjects you can think of.

biology French football computer science painting
physics literature IT chemistry volleyball

Technology **Arts** **Sciences** **Sports**

3 What would you like to learn in these subjects?

History	Maths	Music
English	Geography	Literature
Art	PE	Food technology

Project

Write your ideal school timetable like the one above.

- Choose the lessons you want to learn.
- You can plan one day – or the whole week!
- Choose the subjects you want to study in Technology/Arts/Sciences/Sports.
- Then choose the actual lessons (e.g. the 20th Century / the 1960s / the Middle Ages in History). Write a short description of the lesson.
- Find or draw a classroom picture – or take your own photo!
- Use your imagination – there's a lot to learn!

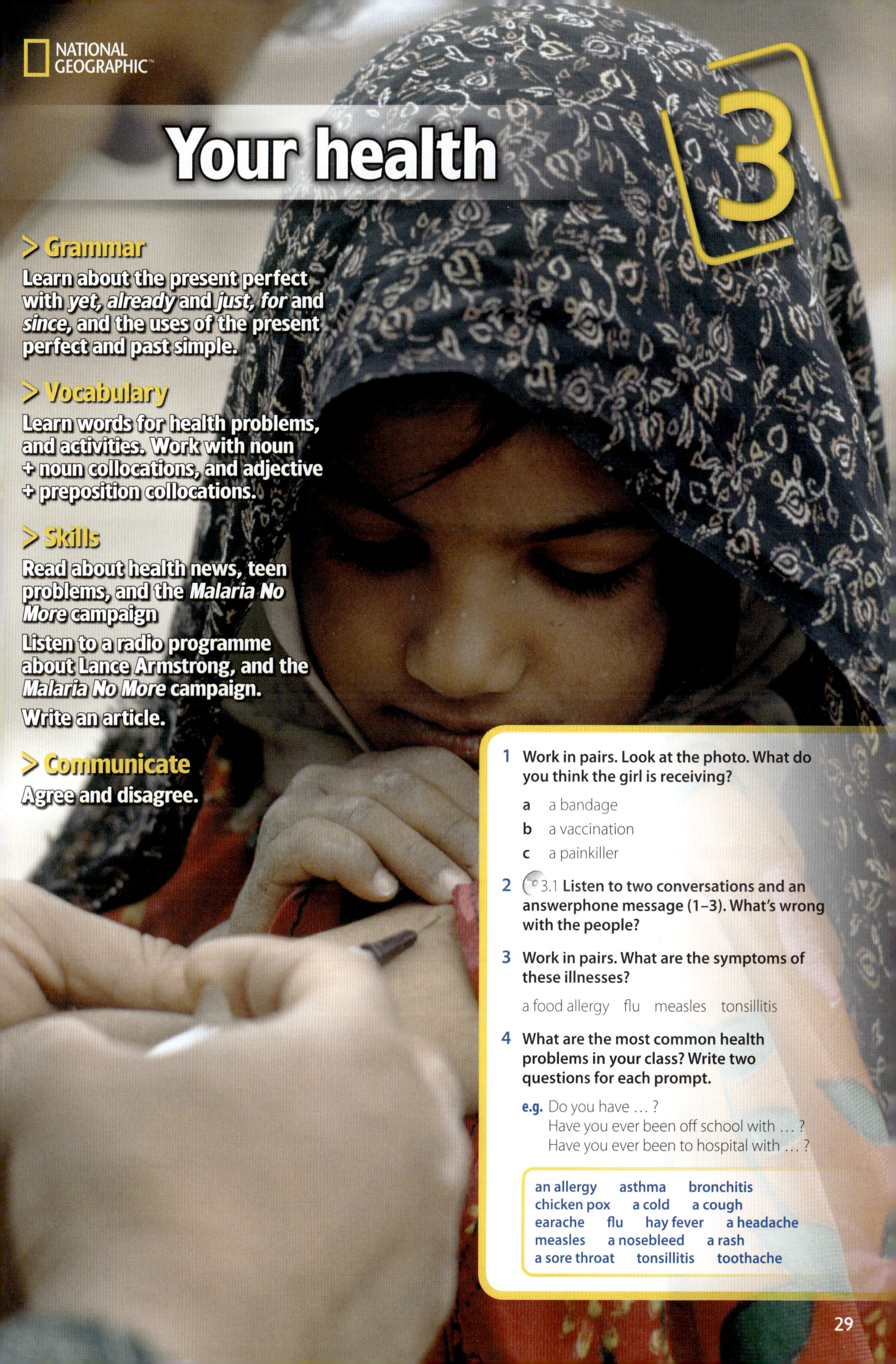

Your health 3

> Grammar

Learn about the present perfect with *yet, already* and *just, for* and *since,* and the uses of the present perfect and past simple.

> Vocabulary

Learn words for health problems, and activities. Work with noun + noun collocations, and adjective + preposition collocations.

> Skills

Read about health news, teen problems, and the *Malaria No More* campaign

Listen to a radio programme about Lance Armstrong, and the *Malaria No More* campaign.

Write an article.

> Communicate

Agree and disagree.

1 **Work in pairs. Look at the photo. What do you think the girl is receiving?**

a a bandage
b a vaccination
c a painkiller

2 3.1 **Listen to two conversations and an answerphone message (1–3). What's wrong with the people?**

3 **Work in pairs. What are the symptoms of these illnesses?**

a food allergy flu measles tonsillitis

4 **What are the most common health problems in your class? Write two questions for each prompt.**

e.g. Do you have … ?
Have you ever been off school with … ?
Have you ever been to hospital with … ?

an allergy asthma bronchitis
chicken pox a cold a cough
earache flu hay fever a headache
measles a nosebleed a rash
a sore throat tonsillitis toothache

3A Health news

The Daily news

A

Have you had flu yet this winter? Why do more people get flu in winter than in summer? This fact has puzzled scientists for many years. But a new study has just shown that the flu virus prefers the cold, dry air in winter. Perhaps this means that the usual advice for treating flu symptoms is correct: stay warm and drink a lot of liquids. And remember: take painkillers, not antibiotics, for viral illnesses!

C

Are you travelling abroad for your holidays this year? Have you had all your vaccinations yet? According to doctors, the number of holidaymakers returning to the UK with tropical diseases has increased. One doctor said, 'I've seen five people with hepatitis since March. That's very unusual. People should take tablets and get vaccinations before they travel.'

B

You probably like the taste of honey, but have you ever put it on your skin? A London hospital has just announced a new treatment for cuts, burns and skin infections, using honey bandages. The usual treatment with antibiotics often doesn't work because many bacteria have become resistant to antibiotics. However, honey kills bacteria. The hospital has used the new bandages for a week and they have already had excellent results.

D

Be careful! The poison from this beautiful cone snail is strong enough to kill you. Several people have already died from its sting because scientists haven't found a cure yet. However, doctors have known for a long time that some poisons can be useful. Now, they have developed a painkiller and a medicine for epilepsy from the cone snail's poison.

Reading and listening

1 **Read the news stories quickly. Match the headlines (1–5) with the stories (A–D). There is one extra headline.**

1. Honey makes your skin healthy
2. An answer to the flu mystery
3. A new treatment for asthma
4. How can a snail save your life?
5. More tropical illnesses in the UK

2 3.2 **Read and listen to the news stories. Complete the table.**

	illness	cause	prevention or treatment
A	flu	....	stay ...., drink lots of liquids, take ....
B	skin infections	bacteria	.... and ....
C	tropical diseases, ...	–	.... and ....
D	epilepsy	–	....

Working with words: noun + noun

3 **Look at the examples. Which nouns can go before *ache* to give words for health problems?**

flu + virus = flu virus

pain + killer = painkiller

See Working with words: Page 103

Grammar: present perfect with *yet, already* and *just*

4 **Complete the sentences from the news stories.**

1. But a new study has .... shown that the flu virus prefers the cold, dry air in winter.
2. The hospital has used the new bandages for a week and they have .... had excellent results.
3. Have you had all your vaccinations .... ?
4. Several people have already died from its sting because scientists haven't found a cure ....

See Grammar Explorer: Page 119

5 **Choose the correct option.**

We use **already / yet** in *affirmative* sentences.
We use **already / yet** in *questions* and *negatives*.

6 **Look at the picture. Then complete the list with the names. The time now is 13.00.**

Vaccination times			
....	12.40	....	12.55
Philip	12.45	**Mark**	13.00
David	12.50	....	13.05

7 **Put the words in order to make statements and questions.**

1 already / my medicine. / taken / have / I
2 the hospital / you / been to / have / yet?
3 has / my brother / the measles. / already / had
4 yet / have not / we / to the nurse. / spoken
5 just / has / my sister / the doctor's. / gone to

> We use *gone to* when a person is in a different place. We use *been to* when the person has come back from the place.

8 **Make statements and questions with the present perfect and *yet* or *already*.**

1 you / speak to the doctor?
2 the nurse / give me some tablets.
3 I / not have / a cold.
4 your mum / recover from her operation?
5 my brother / try the new skin cream.

Grammar: present perfect with *for* and *since*

9 **Read the sentences and choose the correct option (a or b).**

		The sentence refers to ...
1	This fact has puzzled scientists for many years.	a) a period of time b) the start of a period
2	I've seen five people with hepatitis since March.	a) a period of time b) the start of a period

See Grammar Explorer: Page 120

10 **Do we use the expressions in the box with *for* or *since*? Put the words into two groups.**

> one o'clock   a long time   days   a month
> hours   March   Monday   a week   years
> yesterday   21 January   1980

11 **Complete the sentences with *for* or *since*.**

1 My aunt has been in hospital .... Sunday.
2 My dad hasn't been to the doctor's .... ten years.
3 I haven't had an asthma attack .... April.
4 I've taken three painkillers .... eight o'clock.
5 My friend hasn't been to school .... two days.

12 **Complete the conversation with *yet*, *already*, *just*, *for* and *since*.**

Doctor: So, what's the matter with you?
Patient: I feel awful. I've had earache (**1**) .... three days.
Doctor: And have you got any other symptoms?
Patient: Well, I can't hear properly and I've had a headache (**2**) .... yesterday.
Doctor: OK. Have you taken any medicine (**3**) .... ?
Patient: Oh yes, I've (**4**) .... taken a lot of painkillers. And I've (**5**) .... tried some ear drops. That was a few minutes ago.
Doctor: Has anybody checked your ears (**6**) .... ? Let's see ... Oh, what's this? It looks like the earpiece from an MP3 player!

Speaking

13 **Work in pairs. Write a dialogue between a doctor and a patient. Practise the dialogue with your partner.**

Fast finishers

How many past participles do you know? Learn ten new ones today. Then learn ten a day until you know them all.

3B Healthy mind, healthy body

Teen to teen

Do you have a problem? Are you worried about a friend? Send us an email and get help from other teenagers who have had experience of the problem.

1

I'm fed up with my best friend. She's completely changed since her birthday. Her mum gave her a mobile phone. Before, we had a lot of fun together, shopping and meeting friends. Now she spends all her time sending texts on her mobile. She hasn't been out with us for weeks and she's not interested in doing anything. And she's had problems at school because she checks for messages in class. What should I do?

Maria

2

I'm worried about my brother. He eats a lot of junk food. He's already eaten four doughnuts and two packets of crisps today, and it's only 11 a.m. And he's drunk three cans of energy drink. Last night, he told our mum he wasn't hungry, but he went to the shop and bought chocolate. He's always in a bad mood. I tried to talk to him about it, but he got angry with me. In fact, he hasn't spoken to me at all this week. My parents haven't noticed yet. Should I say something to them?

Damon

Reading and listening

1 STUDY SKILLS **Work in pairs. Read the introduction to the webpage. What problems do you think people will write about? Add your ideas to the list.**

- school problems
- bullying
- smoking
- eating problems
- drugs

2 3.3 **Read and listen to the letters. Check your answers to Exercise 1.**

3 3.4 **Read and listen to the replies. Match the replies (A–D) with the letters (1–2). There are two extra replies.**

A

Your brother has a bad habit, and possibly an addiction. Ten per cent of teenage smokers show signs of addiction in the first two days! You should help your brother – join clubs and do healthy activities with him. We did this with my sister, and she stopped smoking.

B

Your friend has a very unhealthy lifestyle. You should help her find an activity she's good at. I started cycling – and I've lost six kilos!

C

Wow! There's a lot of caffeine in three cans of energy drink! Junk food is full of addictive things like sugar, salt, and fat. I changed my diet when I found this out. You should talk to your parents about your brother's problem.

D

Tell your parents about this. Your friend needs help. She can control her addiction. She needs to limit the time her phone is switched on. She should also do other activities, like sports, where she can't use her phone.

Grammar: present perfect and past simple

4 Look at the sentences from the texts. When did these things happen? Match the sentences (1–4) with the times (a–b).

1 Her mum gave her a mobile phone.
2 She's had problems at school.
3 He's drunk three cans of energy drink.
4 He went to the shop and bought chocolate.

a At a finished time in the past.
b During a period of time that includes the present.

See Grammar Explorer: Page 120

5 Complete the sentences with the present perfect or past simple form of the verbs.

e.g. My friend ...hasn't spoken... to me since Monday. (**not / speak**)

1 We .... to the teacher last Monday. (**speak**)
2 My sister .... chocolate for months. (**not / eat**)
3 I .... on a diet last year. (**go**)
4 My dad .... smoking in May. (**give up**)
5 I .... any computer games this week. (**play**)

Working with words: adjective + preposition

6 Look at the examples. Then find the prepositions after *interested* and *angry* in the letters.

I'm fed up with my best friend
I'm worried about my brother.

See Working with words: Page 103

Speaking

7 Work in pairs. Imagine a friend has one of the problems in Exercise 1. What advice will you give them? Now compare your ideas with a new partner.

Listening

8 STUDY SKILLS Work in pairs. How much do you know about the cyclist Lance Armstrong? Compare your ideas with another pair.

9 3.5 Listen to the radio programme and check your ideas from Exercise 8.

10 3.5 Listen again and choose the best answers.

1 Lance Armstrong .... from cancer.
  a recovered
  b is recovering
  c hasn't recovered
2 Lance says you should stay by …
  a going cycling.
  b doing regular exercise.
  c being strong.
3 Lance says young people should …
  a eat a lot and not smoke.
  b eat junk food sometimes but stop smoking.
  c not start smoking and eat well.

Speaking

11 Put the words in the box into two groups: *healthy* and *unhealthy* activities.

be active do exercise do sports
drink fizzy drinks eat junk food eat well
lose weight meet friends sleep well
smoke stay fit watch a lot of TV

12 Work in pairs. Prepare six questions using the present perfect and the expressions from the vocabulary box in Exercise 11. Then ask and answer the questions.

e.g. A: *Have you eaten any junk food this week?*
B: *Yes, I've had two burgers since Sunday!*

Study skills

Predict and check

Before you read or listen to a text, think about the topic.

1 What do you know about the topic? Write your ideas.
2 Write words in English connected to the topic.
3 When you read or listen, check for your ideas and words.

3C Agreeing and disagreeing

Reading and listening

1 3.6 **Read and listen to the dialogue. Who is going on holiday at Christmas?**

a Lee and Jack **b** Aneta and Lee **c** everyone

2 **Read the dialogue again. Find all the statements where somebody agrees and where somebody disagrees.**

Aneta: These are great photos, Lauren. Ireland looks beautiful and really green. It's not like Poland.
Lauren: Have you been back to Poland recently, Aneta?
Aneta: No, I haven't. I'm going to see my cousins at Christmas.
Lee: So am I. I'm going to China. Where are you going for Christmas, Jack?
Jack: Nowhere. I'm staying at home with my family.
Lauren: Me too. I've never been abroad..
Jack: I have. I've been to France twice. Last year, I went to Spain but I was ill all week. I think it was the sun. Have you ever had sunstroke?
Lee: No, I haven't.
Lauren: Me neither.
Aneta: I have. I had a really high temperature and felt terrible.
Jack: So did I. It was awful!
Aneta: Lee, have you had your vaccinations yet?
Lee: Yes. I had my typhoid injection last week and got a rash all over my body.
Lauren. Poor you! And have you packed your suitcase yet?
Lee: No, I haven't. We don't leave until the middle of December!
Aneta: Neither do I. I also need to buy a new suitcase first.
Lee: I don't. I'm only taking a rucksack. I can buy everything I need in China.
Jack: Make sure you buy lots of insect repellent.
Lee: Don't worry. I'm sure my mum has thought of that! She's really worried about the mosquitoes.

3 **Match the statements (1–5) with the responses (a–e).**

1 I'm from Egypt.
2 I'm not English.
3 I went to France last year.
4 I've been to Spain.
5 I like travelling.

a I don't.
b I haven't.
c Me too.
d Neither am I.
e So did I.

See Grammar Explorer: Page 120

4 3.7 **Listen and repeat the *Useful expressions*. Focus on your intonation.**

USEFUL EXPRESSIONS

Agreeing
So am I.
Me too.
Me neither.
So did I.
Neither do I.

Disagreeing
I have.
I don't.

5 **Complete the dialogue with the correct form of the words in the box.**

be   do   have

Lauren: I've never had a really serious illness.

Jack: Neither (**1**) .... I. But I fell off my bike once and broke my leg.

Lauren: So (**2**) .... I. I was off school for two weeks.

Jack: So (**3**) .... I. It was really boring.

Speaking

6 **Work in pairs. Take turns saying the statements (1–5) and responding. Use *So* … and *Neither* ….**

1 I went to the dentist yesterday.
2 I've never been in hospital.
3 I was ill last week.
4 I don't like taking medicine.
5 I can run fast.

7 **Prepare six statements with the present simple, past simple or present perfect for your partner to agree or disagree with. Use the prompts below or use your own ideas. Then take turns saying your statements and responding.**

go / Italy
have / passport
take / malaria tablets
fly / helicopter
get / sunburnt
like / hot weather

Pronunciation: vowel sounds /æ/ and /ʌ/ in irregular verbs

8 3.8 **Listen and tick the words you hear.**

1 began   begun
2 drank   drunk
3 ran   run
4 sang   sung
5 swam   swum

9 **Practise saying these sentences.**

1 I've never swum in the sea.
2 He sang in the concert last night.
3 Who's drunk all the orange juice?
4 She began playing tennis when she was four.

Writing: an article

1 **Read the article Lauren wrote about Emma Watson for a school competition. Match the topics (a–c) with the paragraphs (1–3).**

a Reason why this person is a good role model.
b Background and achievements.
c Lifestyle.

2 **Find examples of *although*, *even though* and *however* in the article. Which two expressions have the same meaning?**

See Grammar Explorer: Page 120

3 **Choose the correct expression or expressions in each sentence.**

1 Although / Even though / However he had no experience of acting, he was a huge success in his first film.
2 He has a healthy vegetarian diet. Although / Even though / However, he loves chocolate and cake.
3 She goes running every morning although / even though / however she often starts work at 7 a.m.
4 He's always busy. Although / Even though / However, he always has time to help other people.

4 **Write notes about a role model you admire. Use the article and the paragraph headings in Exercise 1 to help you. Then write a short article. Remember to use the linking words from Exercise 2.**

Who do you think is a good role model for young people today, and why?

1

Emma Watson is a young British actress. She is famous for her role as Hermione Granger in the Harry Potter films and has won many acting awards. Although Emma has been very busy filming the Harry Potter films, she has continued to study hard. She left school with excellent grades and went to an American university to study.

2

As well as acting, Emma sings and dances. She is a great hockey player and has been a skier since she was five years old. She recently learned how to scuba dive. She doesn't smoke and she prefers hot chocolate to coffee. She has a healthy diet and enjoys cooking. However, she usually makes cakes and biscuits!

3

I think Emma Watson is an ideal role model for girls because she has got a lot of talent, and she is sporty and academic. She has not become a typical celebrity, even though she has been in the media a lot. Emma Watson is a very confident and energetic person. In interviews, she is always polite, intelligent and friendly.

3D Staying healthy in Africa

Culture

Reading

1 **Work in pairs. What can you see in the photos?**

2 3.9 **Read about the tropical disease malaria in Africa. Match the headings (a–c) with the paragraphs (1–3).**

- **a** The *Malaria No More* campaign
- **b** Theatre with a message in an African village
- **c** Mosquitoes and other problems

3 **Read the text again and find these things.**

1. the cause of malaria
2. two reasons why so many children die from malaria
3. two activities that *Malaria No More* does to fight malaria

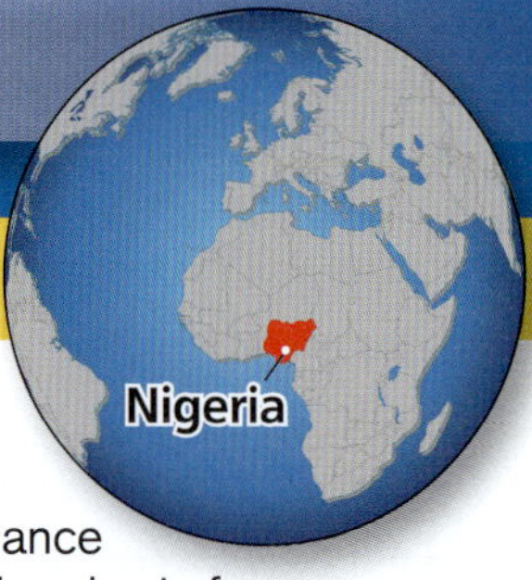

1 In a village in Tanzania, an audience of children and adults is watching a performance by a group of local actors. The play is funny, dramatic and entertaining. However, it also has a serious message – it tells the story of the most dangerous animal in the world, and what happened to a boy when that animal bit him. In many places in Africa, theatre and music bring news and education to isolated villages because it's difficult to buy newspapers or watch TV.

2 So, which animal is the most dangerous in the world? A lion? A shark? What about a mosquito? Mosquitoes carry the parasite that causes malaria and every day malaria kills more than 3,000 children in Africa. Although scientists have developed medicines to treat malaria, they are expensive. And even though there are special insect-repellent nets for people to sleep under, it's difficult for people to get them.

3 The organisation *Malaria No More* gives mosquito nets and malaria drugs to families and it sponsors traditional health education in Africa. And in Europe and the USA, it uses the sports and entertainment industry to raise money for its activities in Africa. Forty million people have seen the special shows on *American Idol* and the campaign has raised enough money to buy fifteen million mosquito nets. Sports celebrities Andy Murray and David Beckham launched the *Malaria No More* UK campaign at Wembley Stadium in London, explaining that we can save a child's life for less than the price of a football.

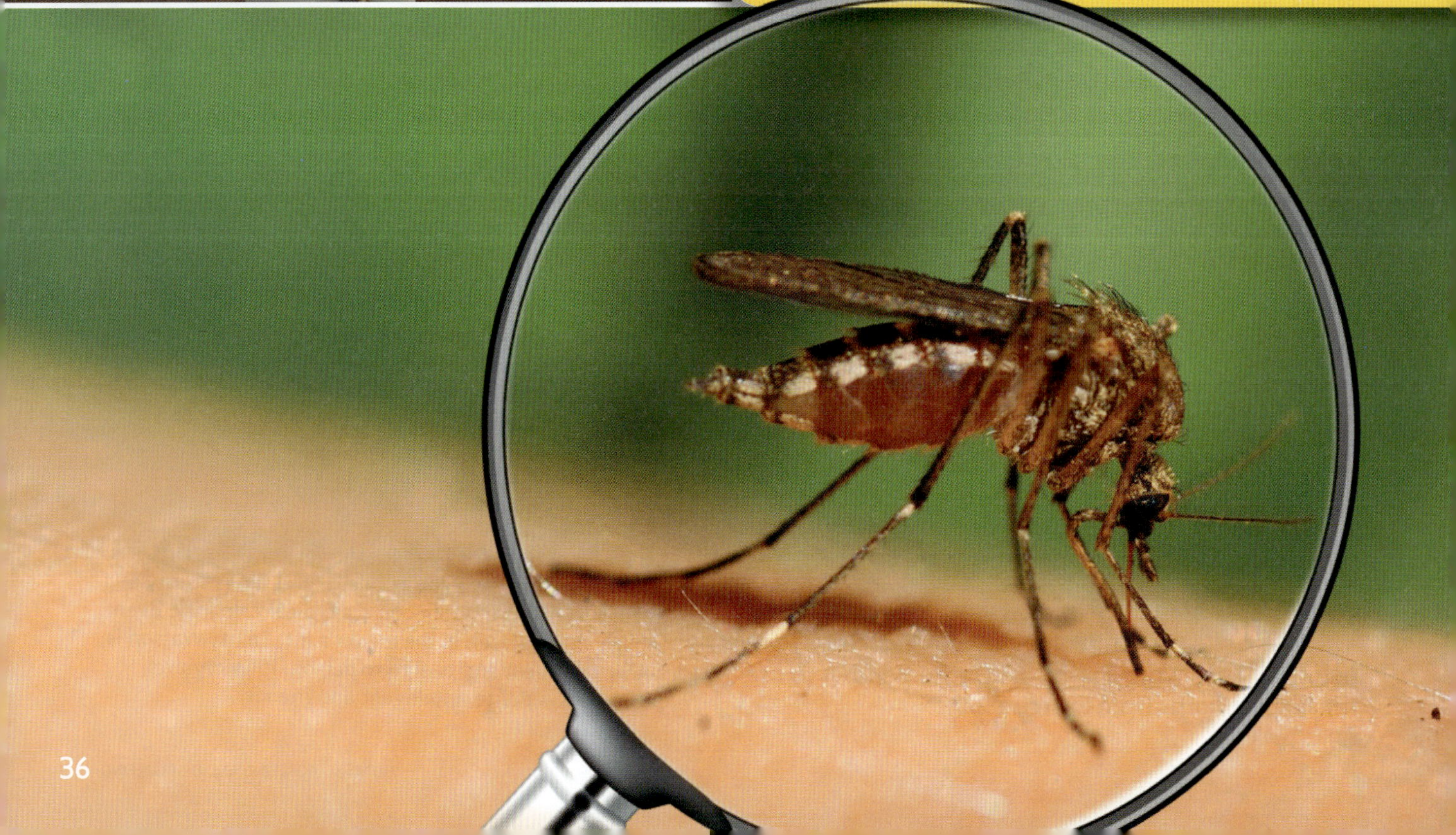

4 **Read the first sentence. Then complete the second sentence so that it gives the same information.**

1 a The actors are performing a play.
  b The actors are giving a ....

2 a There are medicines to treat malaria.
  b Scientists have .... medicines to treat malaria.

3 a Sometimes people can't get mosquito nets.
  b It's .... for people to get mosquito nets.

4 a The shows have had large audiences.
  b A lot of people have .... the shows.

Listening

5 3.10 **Listen to a talk about the *Malaria No More* campaign. What can you do to help?**

6 3.10 **Listen again and complete the notes.**

1 Number of people who die every year from malaria: ....
2 Cost of one bed net: $ ....
3 Ashton Kucher's donation: $ ....
4 The cost of one text donation: $ ....

Biology and English

Blood groups

1 **Work in pairs. Discuss the answers to these questions.**

1 What is blood?
2 How much blood have people got in their bodies?
3 What is a blood donor?

2 **Read the text and find the answers to the questions in Exercise 1.**

What does blood do?

Blood is a kind of transport system. It carries oxygen, carbon dioxide, food and other important substances around the body. There are two kinds of blood cells in the blood. Red blood cells carry oxygen. White blood cells fight infections and diseases.

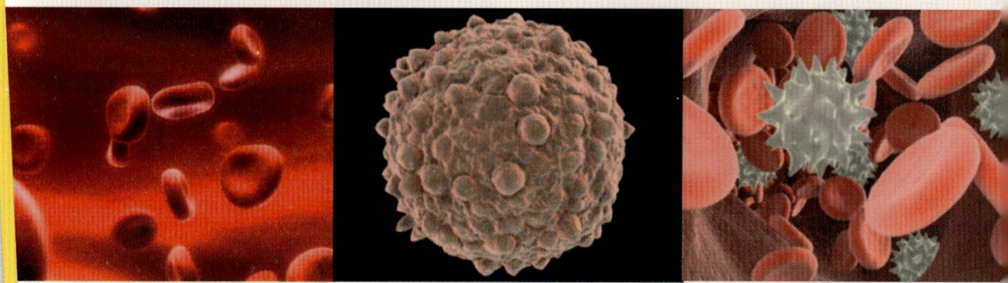

How much blood is there in a human body?

Adults have about five litres of blood. Red blood cells die after about three months, so our bodies make new red blood cells all the time. When people have accidents or operations, they can lose a lot of blood. Their body can't make blood quickly, so they need to get blood from another person.

Is everybody's blood the same?

No, it isn't. There are some small but important differences. In the past, people sometimes died after they received blood from another person (a donor). Nobody understood this until 1901 when the Austrian scientist, Karl Landsteiner, discovered that there are four main types of blood. Some types of blood can mix together in the body without problems, but some combinations become solid and the blood can't move around the body. Landsteiner called the blood types A, B, AB and O.

How many blood groups are there?

Although scientists have identified more than 20 different blood types, Landsteiner's system is still useful today and his discovery has saved millions of lives.

3 **Why was Landsteiner's discovery important?**

Project

Write a health questionnaire for your class. Include questions about lifestyle, illnesses, accidents and blood groups. Present the information in a chart or a poster.

A doctor without borders

TRUE STORY

Christophe Fournier is not a traditional explorer – he usually works in an office for a large organisation. However, Christophe's job can sometimes be just as exciting and dangerous as being an explorer.

Christophe works for *Médecins Sans Frontières* (MSF), an organisation also known as *Doctors Without Borders*. Since 1971, MSF has sent trained doctors all over the world to help people who have suffered from war, disease or disaster. Dr Fournier is a doctor from France who has travelled to many places to organise programs that help people.

At the moment, there are over 27,000 trained medical staff involved in MSF projects and missions. The organisation received the Nobel Peace Prize in 1999.

All kinds of doctors can volunteer for MSF. They need to be prepared to go almost anywhere in the world and, of course, they should expect difficult conditions. Doctors with experience in tropical diseases are particularly useful because most of MSF's work is in Africa, where there are tropical diseases like malaria. When MSF accepts a doctor for a mission, they have to go for at least six months. When doctors have completed a few missions, they might be sent on an emergency mission following a disaster, such as an earthquake.

But why would a doctor leave a comfortable life and a good salary to join MSF? According to Dr Fournier, the experience you gain is a great help in your career. Apart from this, just like the explorers of the past, you need to keep an open mind and learn to mix well with the people you meet. One thing that you can say at the end of any mission is that you have made a real difference to people's lives.

The idea of *Doctors Without Borders* is that people who need medical help should be able to get it, no matter what is going on in their country.

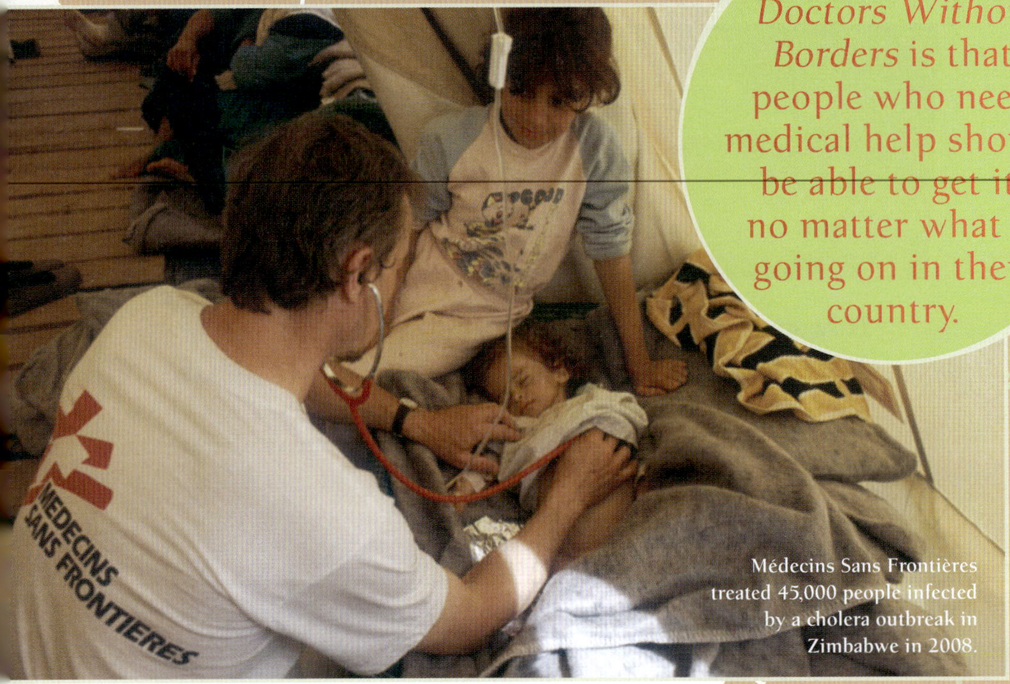

Médecins Sans Frontières treated 45,000 people infected by a cholera outbreak in Zimbabwe in 2008.

MSF have sent doctors to many countries. These are just a few:

- Afghanistan
- Bangladesh
- Cambodia
- Cameroon
- China
- Haiti
- Iran
- Iraq
- India
- Lebanon
- Madagascar
- Malaysia
- Moldova
- Mongolia
- Myanmar
- Pakistan
- Peru
- Poland
- Sierra Leone
- Turkey
- Yemen

1 Read the text and answer these questions with a word or a short phrase.

1. What does Christophe Fournier do?
2. When did MSF begin?
3. What do MSF do?
4. What do doctors who volunteer have to be prepared to do?
5. What do volunteer doctors usually do in Africa?
6. How long must doctors spend on a mission?
7. What do doctors do before they go on an emergency mission?
8. In what ways are volunteer doctors like explorers of the past?

2 Work in pairs. Imagine you are a doctor working for MSF. Take turns telling your partner about your experiences. Use the words in the box.

e.g. *I have been to Africa five times*

go	learn	help	treat	complete	meet	make

Caring for the planet 4

> Grammar

Learn about the present simple and past simple passive with *by*, and quantifiers: all, most, much, many, a lot / lots, some, few, little + nouns.

> Vocabulary

Learn words for natural disasters and wild animals. Work with adjective + noun collocations, and false friends.

> Skills

Read about the environment, the European bison, and symbolic animals.

Listen to an interview about animals, and a journalist talking about elephants.

Write a description of a place.

> Communicate

Give and check information.

1 Work in pairs. Look at the photo. Where do you think it is? Why? Do the natural disasters in the vocabulary box happen in your country?

avalanche	drought	earthquake	flood
hurricane	lightning	mudslide	storm
tornado	tsunami	volcano	wildfire

2 4.1 Listen to four news stories (1–4). Which natural disasters do they describe?

3 4.1 Listen again. Which words do you hear?

ash	fire	land	lava	rain	smoke
snow	temperature	water	wind		

4 Work in pairs. Ask and answer the questions.

1 Which natural disasters are the most frightening / dangerous / destructive? Why?

2 Have you seen any natural disasters on the news? Which ones?

3 Which natural disasters have you experienced? Where? When?

4A The environment

Environment Day

Try our quiz on the natural events and human activities that change our environment. Then calculate your impact on the environment.

1 How are earthquakes caused?
   a) by volcanoes
   b) by tsunamis
   c) by human activity

2 Are volcanoes the most dangerous natural disaster?

3 What's the most important environmental problem today?
   a) floods and fires
   b) pollution from waste
   c) global warming

4 Where do greenhouse gases come from?

1 **a**) and **c**) An earthquake is a violent movement in the Earth's crust. Sometimes, the movement is caused by natural volcanic activity. However, the 2008 Sichuan earthquake in China was caused by human activity – the construction of the Zipingpu dam. On the other hand, tsunamis are often the result of an earthquake under the sea.

2 No. Most volcanoes aren't as destructive as earthquakes. And sometimes, new land is formed by volcanoes. For example, the Canary Islands were created by volcanic eruptions millions of years ago.

3 **c**) It's true that floods and fires destroy enormous areas of land. And the things we throw away, from plastic bags to old computers, don't disappear. Some are recycled, but most are dumped on rubbish tips. But our biggest problem is global warming because every living thing is affected by temperature changes in the environment.

4 In the past, greenhouse gases only occurred naturally. They weren't produced by human activity until the industrial age. The two main sources are burning fuel and deforestation. For example, when trees in the Amazon forest are cut down, the wood is not used. It is burnt. More than 20 per cent of all greenhouse gases are produced as a result of deforestation.

What about you?

In a normal week,

how much …	*how many …*
rubbish does your family throw away?	plastic bags do you use?
plastic does your family recycle?	cans do you throw away?
paper do you waste?	bottles do you recycle?

Calculate your carbon footprint here.

Reading and listening

1 **Work in pairs. Read the questions (1–4) on the webpage. Discuss your answers.**

2 4.2 **Read and listen to the webpage. How many answers did you get right?**

Speaking

3 **Read the last part of the webpage. Discuss your answers with your partner. Think of three things you can do to reduce your carbon footprint – the damage you do to the environment.**

Working with words: adjective + noun

4 Look at the examples. Then find two adjectives before *activity* in the webpage.

natural + disaster = natural disaster

global + warming = global warming

See Working with words: Page 104

Grammar: passive

5 Look at the example. Find more present simple passive verbs in the webpage.

How are earthquakes caused?

The movement is caused by natural volcanic activity.

6 Complete the sentence with the words. What are the causes and the results?

earthquakes tsunamis

.... are caused by ....

We use *by* when we want to say who or what does or causes the action.

7 Complete the table with the words in the box.

is isn't are aren't

Affirmative
It is caused by natural volcanic activity. Many trees (**1**) .... cut down each year.
Negative
The wood (**2**) .... used. Earthquakes (**3**) .... caused by tsunamis.
Questions
(**4**) .... the plastic recycled? How (**5**) .... earthquakes caused?

See Grammar Explorer: Page 121

8 Complete the past simple passive sentences.

1 The earthquake in 2008 .... by human activity. (**cause**)

2 The Canary Islands .... millions of years ago. (**create**)

3 In 2009, 60 per cent of domestic rubbish .... (**not / recycle**)

4 Before 1750, greenhouse gases .... by man. (**not / produce**)

5 When .... plastic .... for the first time? (**make**)

6 .... the trees .... in the hurricane last year? (**blow down**)

9 Choose the correct option.

1 Lightning **kills / is killed** more people than tornadoes.

2 Most avalanches **start / are started** by people.

3 Mount Etna **didn't erupt / wasn't erupted** last year.

4 Trees **cut down / were cut down** to make new farmland.

5 The forest fire **didn't put out / wasn't put out** until the temperature fell.

10 Complete the text with the present simple or past simple passive form of the verbs.

An enormous quantity of oil (**1**) *is needed* (**need**) to produce plastic bags and bottles. In the process, greenhouse gases (**2**) .... (**release**). More than 200 billion litres of bottled water (**3**) .... (**sell**) last year. Most of these bottles (**4**) .... (**not / recycle**) after the water (**5**) .... (**drink**). They (**6**) .... (**throw away**). After many years, plastic waste (**7**) .... (**break down**) into tiny pieces by the weather. Sometimes, it (**8**) .... (**eat**) by birds and other animals. This usually kills them.

Speaking

11 Work in pairs. Use the sentences and question words to make questions in the passive voice.

1 Plastic is made from oil. (**what**)

2 450 million plastic bags are used each month in the UK. (**how many**)

3 Plastic bags were banned in San Francisco in 2007. (**when**)

4 Paper is made from trees. (**what**)

5 One million tonnes of paper are recycled each year in the UK. (**how much**)

6 Paper was invented in China. (**where**)

12 Work with a new partner. Ask and answer the questions from Exercise 11. Take turns.

Fast finishers

Which is the odd one out in each list? Why? Write more lists for a partner.

1 hurricane lightning tornado volcano
2 rain snow water wind
3 ash flood lava smoke
4 gas glass paper plastic

4B Wild animals

The European Bison

The European bison is a symbolic animal. A long time ago, there were bison across western, central and south-eastern Europe and ancient cave paintings are evidence of their importance in the past. Unfortunately, there aren't many wild bison left today. But the story of this magnificent animal is an environmental success story.

Hundreds of years ago, Europe was covered in forest. Then **most** of the trees were cut down and used in construction. (**1**) .... Only a few forests survived but they were full of wild animals such as deer, boar and bison. These animals were hunted for food and for sport. (**2**) .... Bison have **few** predators – only bears, wolves and lynx. In the 19th century these animals were also hunted, so there were **lots of** bison in the forest. Then came the devastation of the First World War. There was **little** food available. **All** of the bison were killed by local people and by the armies. (**3**) .... Two years later, in 1921, the first 'Forestry Reserve' was declared and bison from European zoos were re-introduced to the wild. The objective was to create new herds of bison. Recent data shows that there are now herds of bison in many Eastern-European forests. (**4**) .... Although there isn't much hunting now, these regions are threatened by local commercial interests, urban development and industrial waste.

Reading

1 Read the text and match the sentences (a–e) with the gaps (1–4). There is one extra sentence.

- **a** The last bison was shot in 1919.
- **b** However, the hunting was controlled, and the bison were protected.
- **c** The land was turned into towns and farmland.
- **d** European lynx are an endangered species.
- **e** However, the future of the European bison is still not certain.

Speaking

2 Have you ever seen the animals in the box below? Which ones? Where? Tell your partner.

bat	bear	beaver	bison	boar
deer	eagle	goat	lynx	otter
owl	rabbit	stork	tiger	wolf

3 Work in pairs. Complete the sentences with words from the vocabulary box in Exercise 2. More than one answer is possible.

1 .... fly at night.
2 .... live in rivers and lakes.
3 .... are predators – they eat smaller animals.
4 .... build enormous nests.
5 .... are hunted by wolves.

Listening

4 4.3 **Listen to the interview. What is it about?**

a Hunting wild animals in Europe.
b Reintroducing rare animals into the wild.
c Tracking wild animals in Scotland.

5 4.3 **Listen again. Put the sentences in the correct order.**

a The birds are tracked by satellite.
b The birds were taken to Scotland.
c The adult eagles were released.
d The eagles were kept in a special place.
e The eagles were collected from nests in Norway.

Working with words: false friends

6 Find the words in the text and then choose the correct meanings.

1 objective = **a)** a piece of glass **b)** an idea or intention
2 recent data = **a)** information **b)** the date, e.g. 12 March

See Working with words: Page 104

Grammar: many, much, few, little

7 Look at the examples. Then choose the correct option.

There aren't many wild bison today.
Bison have few predators.
There was little food available.
There isn't much hunting now.

1 We use *many* and *few* with **countable / uncountable** nouns.
1 We use *much* and *little* with **countable / uncountable** nouns.

See Grammar Explorer: Page 121

We often use *much* and *many* in negative sentences and questions.

8 Read the first sentence. Complete the second sentence with *few* or *little*.

1 **a** There weren't many animals in the zoo.
b There were .... animals in the zoo.

2 **a** We didn't have much time.
b We had .... time.

3 **a** We don't have much information.
b We have .... information.

4 **a** I didn't see many people.
b I saw .... people.

9 Choose the correct option.

1 Are there **much / many** endangered species in this country?
2 Scientists found **few / little** bears in the area.
3 How **much / little** snow fell last night?
4 We didn't see **much / many** eagles.
5 **Much / A lot** of the trees in the forest are more than 400 years old.

10 Find the words in the box in the text on page 42. Then use them to complete the table.

few little lots most

100%	all (of) a lot of (**1**) .... (**2**) .... (of)
50%	some (of) (**3**) .... (**4**) ....
0%	no

Speaking

11 Complete the sentence with words from Exercise 10. Then compare with your partner.

1 I've been to .... National Parks.
2 There are .... wild animals where I live.
3 There's .... pollution in our area.
4 There are .... zoos near here.
5 There's .... development in this area.

Study skills

Some English words might look similar to words in your language. This can help you understand a text.

1 When you read, look for words that are similar in both languages.
2 Then read the sentence carefully. Decide if the meaning is similar or if the word is a false friend. There are more similar words than false friends!

4C Giving and checking information

Reading and listening

1 4.4 **Read and listen to the dialogue. What are the subjects of Jack, Lauren and Lee's projects?**

2 **Read the dialogue again. Find the questions. Which questions ask for information? Which questions check information?**

3 **Lee and Jack use three expressions to show they are not sure about things. What are they?**

Lauren: Hi, Jack. Where's Aneta?

Jack: She's in the library. We're doing our science project. We're doing 'Solar power', but I don't know much about it.

Lauren: Oh, neither do I. Do you have to hand it in next week?

Jack: I don't think so. I think it's for the end of term.

Lauren: Is it? My project is for next week.

Jack: What's it about?

Lauren: It's about recycling. Do you know how many recycled bottles are needed to make a jacket?

Jack: I have no idea.

Lauren: Twenty-five.

Jack: Is that possible? Are you sure?

Lauren: Yes, I'm sure … Lee told me. You know he's really into science.

Jack: Oh yes … hey, Lee! What do you know about solar power?

Lee: Actually, I can tell you a lot about solar power. My brother's studying environmental science at university and he's told me a lot about it.

Jack: Really? Is he coming home soon?

Lee: Next week, probably. But I can give you his email address and you can send him a message.

Jack: Great! What's your project, Lee?

Lee: Oh, it's about an animal rescue centre. I've decided to work there at weekends – as a volunteer.

Jack: What about your plans to be a doctor?

Lee: Maybe I'll be a vet instead.

4 4.5 **Listen and repeat the *Useful expressions*. Focus on your intonation.**

USEFUL EXPRESSIONS

What do you know about solar power?
Do you know how many recycled bottles are needed to make a jacket?
Are you sure?
Is that possible?
I can tell you a lot about solar power.
I don't know much about it.
I have no idea.
I don't think so.
Yes, I'm sure.
Next week, probably.
Maybe I'll be a vet instead.

5 **Match the sentences (1–4) with the responses (a–e). There is one extra response.**

1 Are you sure?
2 Can you make plastic from plants?
3 Look at this – a car powered by water!
4 What do you know about recycling?

a I don't know much about it.
b I don't think so.
c Is that possible?
d Yes, I'm sure.
e Pollution, probably.

Speaking

6 **Work in pairs. Talk about the topics in the box. Use the *Useful expressions*. Begin each conversation with *What do you know about … ?***

jazz National Parks pandas
American football India

Pronunciation: the letter 'o' and the vowel sounds /ʊ/, /uː/ and /ʌ/

8 4.6 **Listen and repeat the words in the box.**

blood book cool does flood foot
good move school shoot some wolves

9 4.6 **Listen again and complete the table.**

/ʊ/	/uː/	/ʌ/
book	cool	blood

Writing: a description of a place

1 **Read Jack's article. Then match the topics (a–c) with the paragraphs (1–3).**

a A special place
b General information and history
c Things to do and see

2 **Find *for example, such as, including, also* and *too* in the article.**

See Grammar Explorer: Page 121

3 **Choose the correct option.**

There are many areas of natural beauty in Britain. (**1**) **For example / Such as**, you can visit the Lake District and the Cairngorms, where there are beautiful mountains. Snowdonia, in Wales, is (**2**) **too / also** mountainous. In these places, you can do lots of outdoor activities, (**3**) **like / also** mountain climbing and sailing. You can go hiking (**4**) **such as / too**. There is a lot of accommodation, (**5**) **including / also** camping, chalets, bed and breakfast or hotels.

4 **Write a description of your favourite place. Use Jack's article to help you. Use the linking words in Exercise 2.**

My favourite place: Dovedale

1 Dovedale is a beautiful valley in the Peak District, Derbyshire. Dovedale was formed 350 million years ago from limestone rock. During two ice ages, the rock was cut into strange and amazing shapes by the melting ice, and caves were also formed.

2 There are many things to do and see in Dovedale. For example, you can go hill walking or trout fishing in the River Dove. You can visit the caves too. In the past, many of the caves, such as Reynard's Cave, were used as shelters. There is also a lot of wildlife, including rare plants and birds. In 2006, Dovedale became a National Nature Reserve.

3 My favourite part of Dovedale is the Stepping Stones. During the summer, when the water is low, you can cross the stones or paddle in the river. It's a great place for a picnic, and to relax and enjoy the scenery.

4D Animals in India

Reading

1 Work in pairs. Which words in the box below can you use to describe the animals in the photos? Use a dictionary.

dangerous	domesticated	endangered	
pets	protected	sacred	symbolic	wild

2 4.7 Work in pairs. Do you think these sentences are true or false? Why? / Why not? Then read about animals in India.

1 Elephants are wild animals found in Africa.
2 Cows live on farms and they produce milk and meat.
3 Tigers are common in Asia.

3 Read the text again. Find three reasons why these animals are important in Indian life.

Culture

India is a huge country with many different types of habitat, including deserts, forests and the highest mountains in the world – the Himalaya. It has over 65,000 species of animals, such as elephants, rhinos and bears. And it is the only country in the world with both lions and tigers.

Animals are important in Indian culture and some are treated in a special way. For example, a lot of the elephants aren't wild. They are domesticated. They aren't kept as pets but as working animals. Every working elephant has its own carer, a boy called a *mahout*. An elephant and its mahout meet for the first time when they are both young, and they grow up together. In fact, their relationship continues for the rest of the elephant's life – perhaps 40 years. Lots of elephants work in the forest, moving heavy trees when they are cut down. Some give rides to tourists, or they carry people during ceremonies and festivals. Mahouts usually take excellent care of their elephants, feeding them well and giving them a bath at the end of the working day.

Another special animal in India is the cow. Cows are protected animals, so they aren't kept on farms or killed for food although people do use their milk. In the Hindu religion, cows are sacred animals. So in India you can often see cows walking around towns and cities, and nobody tries to control them. If they sit down in the middle of the road, people simply drive around them!

The Bengal tiger is a symbol of strength and health in India – in fact, it's the national animal. However, the tiger population has fallen and now it's an endangered species. Luckily, things are beginning to change: the 'Kids for Tigers' campaign is supported by more than a million children, and the number of tigers in one important park – the Panna Tiger Reserve – has increased.

a

b

4 **Match the adjectives with the nouns. How many more adjectives can you think of to go with *animal*?**

Indian working sacred endangered

animal culture day species

5 **Look at photo A. Then choose the correct options (a, b or c) to complete the text.**

The elephant in the photo is coming back from a festival. He is wearing a headdress which is (**1**) .... gold and he has bells around his ankles. The elephant is standing (**2**) .... two trainers and another trainer is riding on his back. There is (**3**) .... elephant behind them. The photo was (**4**) .... by a National Geographic photographer.

1	**a**	paint	**b**	painted	**c**	painting
2	**a**	between	**b**	opposite	**c**	in front of
3	**a**	other	**b**	more	**c**	another
4	**a**	took	**b**	take	**c**	taken

Listening

6 4.8 **Listen to a journalist talking about elephants. Where is he?**

a At a temple. **b** At a festival. **c** At a health camp.

7 4.8 **Listen again and choose the correct option (a, b or c).**

1 How long do the elephants stay at Punnathur?
- **a** One day.
- **b** One week.
- **c** One month.

2 Who washes the elephants' faces?
- **a** A junior trainer.
- **b** A senior trainer.
- **c** Another elephant.

3 What do the elephants do after their bath?
- **a** They have dinner.
- **b** They play.
- **c** They go to sleep.

4 Where do these elephants usually live?
- **a** In the jungle.
- **b** In palaces.
- **c** In temples.

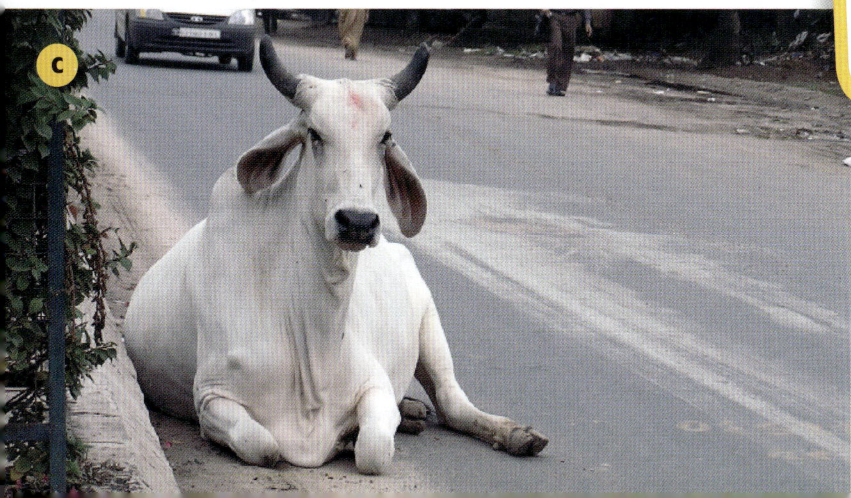

C

Biology and English

Endangered species

1 **Work in pairs. Discuss these questions.**

1 What was the Dodo and what happened to it?

2 Why do animals become endangered?

2 **Read the article and check your answers**

Most people have heard of the Dodo. It lived on the island of Mauritius in the Indian Ocean, and it became extinct in 1681. Why did Dodos disappear? There are several reasons and they are all relevant today, more than 300 years later.

Firstly, the Dodo was a bird, but it was large and heavy, and it couldn't fly. It lost the ability to fly because there were no predators on Mauritius. Secondly, the Dodo wasn't afraid of humans because there weren't any people on Mauritius until 1600. So, when people arrived with monkeys, pigs and other animals, the Dodo's habitat changed very quickly. Dodo nests and eggs were destroyed by the new predators and the adult birds were probably shot or caught. The forest was changed too by people who started to farm the land.

Today, animals are threatened by the same dangers – human activity and habitat destruction. In Asia, people have moved into new areas and there is less wild habitat for tigers. In Africa, changes in the way land is used means that there is much less forest for mountain gorillas. And all around the world, different species are threatened by the effects of climate change, from polar bears in the Arctic to coral reefs on the equator.

3 **Do you think it is important to try and save species from extinction? Why? / Why not?**

Project

Find out about wild animals in your country. What is their natural habitat? Are they protected? Are any of them endangered?

Consolidation Units 3 and 4

Gapped texts

Using the correct word form

- Read the gapped text quickly, once.
- Look at the words given. Decide if they are adjectives, verbs, adverbs or nouns.
- Read each gapped sentence. Decide what changes you must make to the words.
- **Important!** Read the whole text again when you finish.

1 Look at the groups of words. What kind of words are they?

1 small new expensive
2 go be have
3 begin find sell

2 Answer these questions about the groups of words in Exercise 1.

1 What are the comparative forms?
2 What are the past simple forms?
3 What are the past participles of the verbs?

3 Now look at this task. What changes must you make to the words in the box?

be go have

Hi David,
I'm sorry I wasn't at home when you came. I (**1**) .... to visit my sister in hospital. She has (**2**) .... there since Monday. She (**3**) .... her baby on Tuesday!
Jenny

4 Complete the gapped text with the correct form of the words in the box.

bad buy have

Dear Mark,
I'm sorry we (**1**) .... an argument last night. I was in a really bad mood. This has been the (**2**) .... week of my life! I've decided to make some changes. I (**3**) .... you a present – it's in your bedroom. See you later.
Andrew

Reading

Understanding the organisation of a text

- Read the whole text quickly.
- Read the additional sentences.
- Read carefully the sentences before and after the first gap.
- Make sure the grammar also matches.
- Repeat for each gap.

1 Read the sentences. What topic have they got in common?

a The resort is opening new ski runs this winter.
b He has skied on every mountain in Europe.
c They were all experienced skiers.

2 Read the text quickly. Choose the best option.

Skiing disasters on Europe's mountains
2009 was a bad year for avalanches in the Alps. Three skiers were killed in separate accidents in France and Switzerland. (**1**) .... Scientists say the avalanches were caused by sudden increases in temperature.

a Skiing accidents that happened in 2009
b A famous European skier
c A new ski resort in France

3 Which sentence from Exercise 1 fits the gap?

4 Read the text and match the sentences (a–c) with the gaps (1–2). There is one extra sentence.

Many homeless after earthquakes.
There were several major earthquakes last year. (**1**) .... In Japan, two large cities in the north of the country were affected. Many buildings were destroyed. People have moved to other areas to look for new homes. (**2**) .... Scientists say more earthquakes are expected.

a Some have gone to live with their families in other parts of Japan.
b Volcanoes often erupt at this time of year.
c They hit countries including China and Japan.

Present perfect and past simple with *for* and *since*

We use *for* and *since* with the present perfect. We can also use *for* with the past simple.

1 Complete the sentences with *for* or *since*.

1 I've played tennis four times .... May.
2 We played tennis .... two hours, then we went swimming.
3 I haven't played tennis .... three weeks. Let's have a game.
4 My sister is a vegetarian. She hasn't eaten meat .... five years.
5 My mum hasn't smoked .... New Year's Eve.
6 My dad smoked .... ten years.

Present perfect and past simple with time expressions

We use the past simple with time expressions for a finished time in the past.

We use the present perfect with time expressions for a period of time that includes the present.

2 Choose the correct verb forms.

1 I **didn't watch / haven't watched** TV last week.
2 We **went / have been** to the doctor's twice this month.
3 My friend **broke / has broken** his leg yesterday.
4 I **wasn't / haven't been** ill last year.
5 We **did / have done** lots of exercise this week.

3 Choose the correct option.

1 We've done a lot of cycling **this year / last year**.
2 I've been ill **on Monday / since Monday**.
3 We saw two eagles **in June / since June**.
4 I didn't go to the park **last Sunday / since Sunday**.
5 We were here **at one o'clock / since one o'clock**.

4 Write the sentences in Exercise 3 with the second time expression. Change the verb forms.

Present perfect and past simple without time expressions

Sometimes we don't use a time expression. The time period is clear from the information we give.

5 Read the sentences and decide if the time period is in the past or includes the present. Then choose the correct option.

1 John Lennon **was / has been** an incredible musician.
2 Nelly Furtado **made / has made** some great albums.
3 Michael Phelps **won / has won** eight gold medals at the Beijing Olympics.

6 Write the correct form of the verbs: present perfect or past simple.

Alexander Fleming (**1**) .... (**win**) the Nobel prize in 1945. He (**2**) .... (**discover**) the antibiotic, penicillin. Since then, scientists (**3**) .... (**develop**) different kinds of antibiotics. Antibiotics (**4**) .... (**save**) many people's lives.

Other uses of the present perfect and past simple

We also use the present perfect when (**a**) we don't know (or say) when something happened.

We use the past simple when (**b**) we ask for or give details (time / place) about something previously referred to or (**c**) we talk about a sequence of events.

7 Find the present perfect and past simple in the dialogue. Match the sentences with the uses (a, b and c) above.

Eva: I've made some popcorn. Do you want some?
Jo: Oh, yes please. I've never made popcorn in my life! How did you make it?
Eva: I put the packet in the microwave for 30 seconds! Then I opened the packet and emptied in into the bowl.
Jo: It seems easy!
Eva: Yes, it is. And you can eat as much as you want because it has no calories.

8 Complete the dialogue with the present perfect or past simple of the verbs.

Eva: (**1**) .... (**take**) you ever this painkiller, AcheAway?
Jo: Yes, I (**2**) .... (**take**) one when I (**3**) .... (**have**) earache last month.
Eva: (**4**) .... (**help**) it ?
Jo: Well, I (**5**) .... (**make**) some hot chocolate, (**6**) .... (**take**) the tablet and (**7**) .... (**fall**) asleep. When I (**8**) .... (**wake up**) , I (**9**) .... (**feel**) better.

Review Units 3 and 4

Vocabulary

1 Complete the dialogue.

A: I feel awful. I've got (**1**) a h............. , (**2**) a s............. t............. and (**3**) e............. .

B: Maybe it's (**4**) the f............. . You should take (**5**) a p............. .

1 mark per item: .../5 marks

2 Write the activities.

My family is very healthy. We eat (**1**) w............. and we do (**2**) e............. every day. We're very (**3**) a............. . And we don't (**4**) s............. or eat (**5**) j............. f............. .

1 mark per item: .../5 marks

3 Complete the sentences with words about the environment.

1 A v............. has erupted in Italy.
2 After no rain, there was a d............. .
3 Cars and traffic cause p............. .
4 Things we throw away are r............. .
5 Global w............. is a big problem.

1 mark per item: .../5 marks

4 Write the animals.

1 ....
2 ....
3 ....
4 ....
5 ....

1 mark per item: .../5 marks

5 Complete the sentences.

1 I'm not afraid .... spiders.
2 My friend's really bad .... maths.
3 At our school, ... is from twelve thirty to one o'clock.
4 Lions and tigers are .... animals.
5 My best .... 's name is Katy.

1 mark per item: .../5 marks

Grammar

6 Make statements and questions with the present perfect.

1 I / just / arrive home.
2 you / take the medicine / yet?
3 we / already / see two eagles.
4 your dad / speak to the doctor / yet?
5 I / already / eat my lunch.

1 mark per item: .../5 marks

7 Complete the sentences with *for* or *since*.

1 I haven't been to the doctor's .... last year.
2 My friend has lived here .... a month.
3 My mum has been a vegetarian .... 1998.
4 I've read two books .... yesterday.
5 My dad hasn't smoked .... March.

1 mark per item: .../5 marks

8 Complete the sentences with the present perfect or past simple form of the verbs.

1 I .... any fizzy drinks today. (**not / drink**)
2 I .... a cold in January. (**have**)
3 We .... two exams this week. (**do**)
4 Mount Etna .... three times last summer. (**erupt**)
5 My friend .... ill since Monday. (**be**)

1 mark per item: .../5 marks

9 Complete the sentences with the passive form of the verbs.

1 Glass bottles .... in our town. (**recycle**)
2 Plastic .... from oil. (**make**)
3 The area .... by a tsunami in 2006. (**destroy**)
4 The species .... until 2009. (**not / discover**)
5 All the tickets .... last week. (**sell**)

1 mark per item: .../5 marks

10 Choose the correct option.

1 There **was / were** few animals in the forest.
2 There weren't **many / much** people at the concert.
3 We saw **much / lots of** bison.
4 **Was / Were** there any pollution in the river?
5 There are **few / little** endangered species in the area.

1 mark per item: .../5 marks

Communicate

11 Complete the responses.

1 'I like cycling.'
'Me ....'

2 'I can speak English.'
'So .... I.'

3 'I don't smoke.'
'Me ....'

4 'I was ill yesterday.'
'So .... I.'

5 'I've never seen a lion.'
'Neither .... I.'

2 marks per item: .../10 marks

12 Match the sentences (1–5) with the responses (a–e).

1 What do you know about eagles?
2 This is a solar-powered computer.
3 I need some information on recycling.
4 Are you sure?
5 How do you make popcorn?

a I have no idea.
b Yes, I'm sure.
c I don't know much about them.
d Is that possible?
e I can tell you a lot about it.

2 marks per item: .../10 marks

13 Is the sound the same or different from *run*?

1 come
2 drunk
3 cool
4 blood
5 move
6 book
7 sung
8 good
9 shoot
10 flood

1 mark per item: .../10 marks

14 Match the first parts of the sentences (1–5) to the second parts (a–e).

1 Although I like chocolate,
2 The park has wild animals,
3 Although I studied a lot,
4 We recycle everything,
5 There's lots to do,

a I don't often eat it.
b I failed the exam.
c including paper.
d like sailing and climbing.
e like wolves and bears.

2 marks per item: .../10 marks

15 Complete the paragraph using the words in the box.

all of also even though
for example however lots of
no such as than too

There are (**1**) .... things we can do for the environment. (**2**) .... , we can recycle (**3**) .... the glass we use. We can recycle plastic (**4**) .... We can (**5**) .... buy recycled products, (**6**) .... paper. (**7**) .... recycling uses energy, it's better (**8**) .... using new resources. (**9**) ...., the most important thing is to consume less. We have (**10**) .... alternative.

1 mark per item: .../10 marks

Total: .../100

I can...

I can agree and disagree.
I can give information.
I can check information.

Environment article

England: a country in danger?

A few hundred years ago, 90% of the trees in England were cut down, mostly for houses or for ships that were used to fight wars. Naturally, this led to many animals losing their homes. Today the threat of extinction to animals and plants is still very real.

1 One effect of war on England was that …
   a trees were needed to build ships.
   b houses were destroyed by the enemy.
   c many animals were killed by bombs.

2 The threat to nature in England …
   a is not as serious for animals as it was.
   b is more serious for plants than for animals.
   c could mean that animals and plants will become extinct.

Wildlife

The danger to wildlife in England often comes from human activity, such as urban development or modern farming practices. The large numbers of fish we catch have endangered several species of fish too. Global warming is another great threat to nature. For example, many birds can no longer find food in England, so they move further north to Scotland where it's cooler. But if Scotland also gets warmer, these birds will have nowhere else to go as they can't fly across the sea.

3 Which of the following has not had a bad effect on wildlife?
   a Towns getting bigger.
   b Growing food in gardens.
   c Over-fishing the seas.

4 What do we understand about birds in this paragraph?
   a The food they like can only be found in England.
   b They don't like warm conditions and they can't fly far over water.
   c Their movements are the same as they were thousands of years ago.

Natural disasters

The most devastating natural disasters in England are weather-related. Storms are quite common. In 1987, England was hit by a terrible storm which blew down millions of trees. England doesn't get hurricanes though. Droughts, however, are surprisingly common considering how often it rains in England!

5 Which of the following do not happen in England?
   a Hurricanes.
   b Storms.
   c Droughts.

6 What does the writer say about the rain in England?
   a It is rare.
   b There is a lot of it.
   c It is linked to tsunamis.

Action!

There are very many organisations which protect wildlife. However, individuals and house-owners are making a difference too. Something simple, such as leaving a patch of long grass in your garden for insects, can help keep the balance of nature. There is less that can be done to protect against natural disasters, but many projects to try to keep the number of human casualties to a minimum.

7 What do we understand about insects from the text?
   a They like long grass.
   b They eat a balanced diet.
   c House-owners do more for them than organisations.

8 What does the work on natural disasters focus on?
   a Preventing them from happening.
   b Stopping them from killing people.
   c Keeping people busy with projects.

1 Read the article and answer the questions.

2 Write notes about your country. What could you say about …

the changing environment?
wildlife?
natural disasters?
the action being taken to help?

Project

Write an environment article about your country.

- Find or draw a map of your country and find suitable photos
- Find out about the environment in your country (ask people or use the Internet)
- Write about wildlife
- Write about natural disasters
- Write about the action people are taking

NATIONAL GEOGRAPHIC

Family life

5

> Grammar

Learn about permission and obligation, relative pronouns and relative clauses, reflexive pronouns (*himself*, etc.) and *each other*.

> Vocabulary

Learn words for appearance, and adjectives to describe emotions and feelings. Work with compound adjectives and phrasal verbs for relationships.

> Skills

Read about teenagers and their families, families in China, and multicultural Canada.

Listen to a Chinese-American student talking about China, and a chat-show programme.

Write a description of a person.

> Communicate

Talk about problems.

1 Look at the photo. Do you think these people are friends or relations?

2 5.1 Listen to three conversations (1–3). Which of the names below do you hear?

Penelope Cruz   Hilary Duff   Johnny Depp
Michael Phelps   Cristiano Ronaldo   Venus Williams

3 Think of a famous person or someone your partner knows. Describe the person. Can your partner guess the name? Use the words in the vocabulary box to help you.

dreadlocks   dyed hair   earrings   jewellery
make-up   nail varnish   a necklace   pierced ears
a ring   spikey hair   a stud   a tattoo

5A Me and my family

Aisha

'I love them, but they're a bit old-fashioned. I mean, they don't let me wear make-up or nail varnish on school days. And I'm not allowed to have dyed hair or wear high-heeled shoes. I can go out with my best friend, but they make her come in and chat for half an hour! My dad's so embarrassing! We can't stay out after 10 pm and I have to phone them if I'm five minutes late. My mum's more easy-going than my dad – he's unbelievable!'

Josh

'I get on really well with her. We both love fashion, even though she's always elegant and well-dressed and I'm into new-age stuff. I love going clothes shopping with her – she lets me buy anything I want. She's really open-minded. I mean, I've got dreadlocks and a pierced tongue, but she doesn't mind. We talk to each other about everything – I don't have to worry about shocking her. She tells really funny stories about herself when she was my age. It cheers me up if I'm feeling a bit bad-tempered.'

Colin

'He's so annoying. He's the most self-centred person I know. He's so vain – he's always looking at himself in the mirror. OK, he's quite good-looking – you know, he's a blue-eyed, blond-haired type, but honestly! When we were younger, we had to share a bedroom. We argued about everything. We still do. Now, he has a list of rules on his bedroom door: you must knock on the door before you go in, you mustn't touch his things, you mustn't borrow his clothes... . Crazy!'

Speaking

1 Work in pairs. Discuss the questions.

1. Who do you get on with in your family? Why?
2. Who do you argue with? What about?

Reading and listening

2 Read the texts quickly. Which relation is each person talking about? There is one extra option.

a brother   cousins   a grandmother   parents

3 5.2 **Read and listen to the texts. Find the adjectives which describe the relations. Then put the adjectives into two groups: *appearance* and *personality*.**

e.g. appearance: elegant, well-dressed

4 Use some of the adjectives from Exercise 3 to describe people in your family. Write at least five sentences.

e.g. My parents are easy-going.

Working with words: compound adjectives

5 **Look at the examples. Then find more compound adjectives in the texts.**

They're a bit old-fashioned.
She's always well-dressed.

See Working with words: Page 105

Grammar: permission and obligation

6 **Look at the texts and complete the table.**

Permission to do things
I .... go out with my best friend. We .... stay out after 10 pm. Can you wear earrings at school?
Obligation to do / not to do things
I .... phone them. We .... share a bedroom. You .... knock on the door. You .... touch his things. Do you have to go home before 10 pm?
No obligation to do things
I don't .... worry.

See Grammar Explorer: Page 122

The past simple of *must* is *had to*.

7 **Read the sentences from the texts and choose the correct option (a, b or c).**

1 **They don't let me** wear make-up.
 a I can b I can't c I must
2 **I'm not allowed to** have dyed hair.
 a I can b I can't c I must
3 **They make her** come in and chat.
 a She can b She can't c She must
4 **She lets me** buy anything I want.
 a I can b I can't c I must

See Grammar Explorer: Page 122

8 **Rewrite the sentences with the words in brackets.**

1 I can't wear nail varnish. (**my mum / let**)
2 We can't wear jeans at school. (**allowed**)
3 I can stay out late at the weekend. (**my parents / let**)
4 I have to do my homework before I go out. (**my dad / make**)
5 Can you invite friends around? (**allowed**)

9 **Look at the pictures. In pairs, ask and answer questions using the verbs in the box.**

be allowed to can have to let make

A: *Do you have to wear a uniform at your school?*
B: *Yes, we do. / No, we don't.*

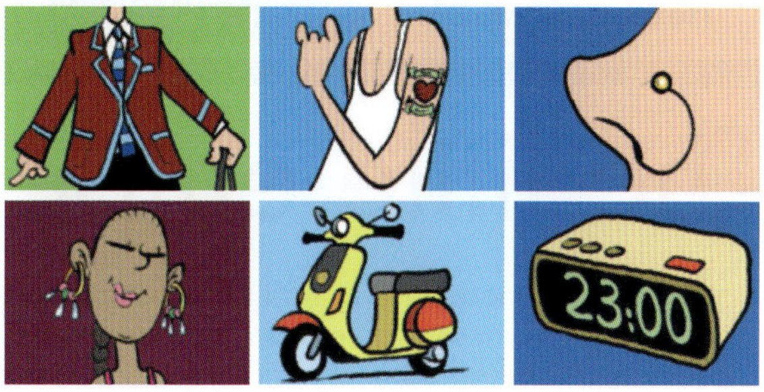

Grammar: reflexive pronouns (*himself*, etc.) and *each other*

10 **Complete the sentences from the texts.**

1 We talk to .... about everything.
2 She tells really funny stories about .... when she was my age.

See Grammar Explorer: Page 123

11 **Complete the sentences with words from the box or *each other*.**

myself yourself herself himself itself ourselves yourselves themselves

1 I looked at .... in the mirror.
2 The sisters get on well with ....
3 We haven't spoken to .... since Monday.
4 Did you enjoy .... at the party?
5 Self-centred people think only about ....

Speaking

12 **What kind of rules are there in your family? Tell your partner. Use the ideas in the box.**

clothes computers food friends going out jobs money TV

A: *My mum doesn't let us eat in front of the TV.*
B: *Oh, I can do that. But I'm not allowed to make a mess!*

Fast finishers

How many different words do you know for these things?

hair colour hairstyles eye colour personal style

5B Families in China

Home | Animals | People and Places | Activities | Videos

Search

The little emperors

Traditionally, Chinese families had lots of children. Everyone looked up to and obeyed the father. But Chinese families have changed. In 1979, the Chinese government took a decision which had a big impact on society. It was a time when the government was worried about the population increase. Now Chinese families can't have more than one child. Most of the teenagers in the big cities are only children.

Teenagers who have no brothers or sisters can feel lonely. 'If you feel annoyed with your friends, you can't fall out with them because there's nobody else to talk to at home,' says one girl. 'I broke up with my boyfriend, but I had nobody to go out with, so we made up again.' In many cities there are few sports centres or places where teenagers can get together. Boys spend the evening in internet cafes, instead of socialising. The cafés have broadband connections which are fast and cheap, and addiction to online gaming is a problem.

On the other hand, many Chinese teenagers say they feel independent and self-confident. They don't let other people, including their parents, take decisions for them. Only children get lots of attention from their parents and their grandparents. Each child has six adults looking after them! They get the best food and clothes. Most of them go to extra English classes after school. Parents who have only one child usually have more money to spend on these things. The children are under pressure to do well, because education and success are important in Chinese society. In fact, these only children are called 'little emperors' because now, in Chinese families, they are the people who everybody must obey and respect.

Listening

1 **How much do you know about China? Make notes for two minutes. Then compare your notes with your partner's.**

2 5.3 **Listen to Jin, a Chinese-American student. Does he talk about the things in your notes?**

3 5.3 STUDY SKILLS **Listen again and choose the correct options (a, b or c).**

1 What's the population of China?
  a 1 million **b** 1.3 billion **c** 3.3 billion

2 How many Chinese people live in cities?
  a 13 per cent **b** 30 per cent **c** 70 per cent

3 How long is the Great Wall of China?
  a 400km **b** 6000km **c** 6400km

4 What colour means good luck to the Chinese?
  a White **b** Red **c** Blue

5 When were the Beijing Olympic Games?
  a 2007 **b** 2008 **c** 2009

Reading and listening

4 **Read the text quickly. Who are 'the little emperors'?**

5 5.4 STUDY SKILLS **Read and listen. Are the sentences true or false?**

1. Chinese families have become smaller since 1979.
2. In Chinese cities, teenage boys play a lot of sports.
3. Chinese families don't have much money to spend on their children.

Speaking

6 **Work in pairs. Do you think Chinese families are similar to families in your country? Why? / Why not?**

Working with words: phrasal verbs for relationships

7 **Look at the examples. Then find six more phrasal verbs in the text.**

You can't fall out with your friends.

I broke up with my boyfriend.

See Working with words: Page 105

Grammar: relative pronouns and relative clauses

8 **Complete the sentences with words from the text.**

1. A person who has no brothers or sisters is an ....
2. A time when most people socialise is the ....
3. A place where teenagers play online games is an ....
4. Two things which are important in Chinese society are .... and ....

See Grammar Explorer: Page 123

9 **Look at the example. Then find the relative pronouns and the relative clauses in the text.**

e.g. The Chinese Government took a decision <u>which had a big impact on society</u>.

We can use *that* instead of *who* or *which* in the sentences in the text.

10 **Complete the sentences with *who, which, where* or *when*.**

1. An emperor is a man .... rules a country.
2. Joe's Cafe is a place .... we can meet our friends.
3. The connection .... is the fastest is broadband.
4. The girl .... broke up with her boyfriend was lonely.
5. The 1970s was a time .... many things changed.
6. The teenagers .... have got the most money are only children.

11 **Choose the correct options (a, b or c) to complete the text.**

A family tree is a kind of diagram (**1**) .... explains your family. It shows the relationships (**2**) .... connect people, for example parents and children. The tree shows (**3**) .... people were born. There are different spaces (**4**) .... the people's names are written. Each generation is written on the same line. Your ancestors – the people (**5**) .... came before you – are at the top of the tree.

1	a which	b who	c where
2	a who	b that	c when
3	a that	b which	c when
4	a that	b where	c which
5	a which	b who	c when

Speaking

12 **Work in pairs. Are the adjectives in the box + (positive) or – (negative)?**

annoyed anxious cheerful confident disappointed embarrassed excited lonely pleased upset

13 **When do you feel annoyed or anxious? Tell your partner. Give details of the situations. Try to use all the words in the box in Exercise 12.**

A: *I feel anxious before an exam.*

B: *Me too! Especially when I haven't studied.*

Study skills

Specific information

1. Before you listen to or read a text, read the questions carefully.
2. Decide what kind of information you need to find: a number, a date, a fact, etc.
3. When you listen to or read the text, focus only on finding that information.

5C Talking about problems

Reading and listening

1 **Look at the photo. Do you think Aneta is feeling upset, anxious or excited?**

2 5.5 **Read and listen to the dialogue. Check your answers to Exercise 1.**

3 **Read the dialogue again. Complete the expressions Jack uses to show interest or surprise.**

1 I .... !
2 Tell ....
3 Go .... !

Jack: Hey, Aneta. What's wrong?
Aneta: I've fallen out with Lee!
Jack: I can't believe that! You get on really well.
Aneta: Not now!
Jack: Calm down. Tell me about it. What happened?
Aneta: Well … last night, we were studying at my house and then, suddenly, Lee looked at me and said …
Jack: Go on! What did he say?
Aneta: He … he wants to go out with me!
Jack: That's not so bad.
Aneta: Yes, it is. Lee's my best friend. I don't want a boyfriend! Anyway, we argued and then he left without saying goodbye.
Jack: Have you made up yet?
Aneta: No. He hasn't spoken to me all day!
Jack: Look, Aneta, it's not the end of the world.
Aneta: It is! Now we can't be friends.
Jack: He's probably upset and confused at the moment. I can talk to him.
Aneta: Good idea. He usually listens to you.
Jack: Cheer up! I'm still your friend. And Lauren is too!
Aneta: Yeah, I know. Thanks, Jack.

4 5.6 **Listen and repeat the *Useful expressions*. Focus on your intonation.**

USEFUL EXPRESSIONS

What's wrong?
I can't believe that!
Calm down.
Tell me all about it.
Go on! What did he say?
That's not so bad.
Cheer up!
It's not the end of the world.

5 **Read Lee's comments. Choose the best responses.**

1 I think Aneta's got a new boyfriend.
 a What's wrong?
 b I can't believe that!

2 Aneta doesn't want to go out with me.
 a Good idea.
 b Cheer up! It's not the end of the world.

3 I think I'm in love with Aneta! I feel terrible!
 a Go on! What did she say?
 b Tell me all about it.

Speaking

6 Work in pairs. Choose one of the situations in the box and write a dialogue. Follow the dialogue map to help you.

You've fallen out with a friend.
You've just broken up with your boyfriend/girlfriend.
You haven't passed your exams.
Your best friend is moving away.

Student A	Student B
1 Ask what's wrong.	Answer A's question.
2 Show surprise/interest. Ask another question.	Give more information.
3 Say the situation isn't so terrible.	Disagree with A.
4 Cheer your friend up.	Respond to A's comment.
5 Say something positive.	

7 Take turns. Practise saying the dialogue. Then choose another situation from the box in Exercise 6 and role-play the conversation.

Pronunciation: homonyms with the sound /eə/

8 5.7 Listen to the words in each pair. Is the pronunciation the same or different? Then practise saying the words.

1	cheer	chair
2	pair	pear
3	fair	fare
4	their	there
5	they're	there
6	where	wear
7	hair	here

9 Practise saying these sentences.

1 There's a chair over there.
2 She's wearing a pair of jeans.
3 Their brother has fair hair.

Writing: a description of a person

1 Read Lee's description of his brother. Then match the paragraphs (1–3) to the information in the box below.

his style/clothes his age and what he does
his personality his eyes, hair and skin his build

2 Lee mentions the similarities between himself and Cheng. Find the sentences with *both* and *neither*.

See Grammar Explorer: Page 124

3 Rewrite the sentences below using the words in brackets.

e.g. Cheng and Lee are tall. (**Both of**)
Both of them are tall.

1 Cheng and Lee have got dark hair. (**Both of**)
2 They have got fair skin. (**Both**)
3 They haven't got blue eyes. (**Neither of**)
4 They don't wear an earring. (**Neither of**)
5 They like the same clothes. (**Both**)

4 Choose a person in your family and make notes about them. Say how this person is similar to or different from you. Use the information in Exercise 1. Then write a description.

1 My older brother Cheng is nineteen and he's studying at university in London. He's really clever and confident. He's always cheerful too. He's friendly and helpful, and he always phones or sends me an email every week.

2 We're quite similar in many ways – we're both tall and slim, and we've both got straight, dark hair. Both of us are fair-skinned because we both take after my mum, who's English. Neither of us has got blue eyes. Cheng's eyes are a dark brown. But mine are just a boring brown colour.

3 I like my brother's style. He usually wears trendy T-shirts and so do I! Neither of us wears an earring, but one day Cheng came home with a stud in his nose! My mum was really annoyed, but I think it looks great.

5D Multicultural Canada

Reading

1 Work in pairs. Look at the photos. What can you see?

2 5.8 **Read the text and find the following information.**

1 The official languages of Canada.
2 Places in Canada.
3 Nationalities of people who live in Canada.

Culture

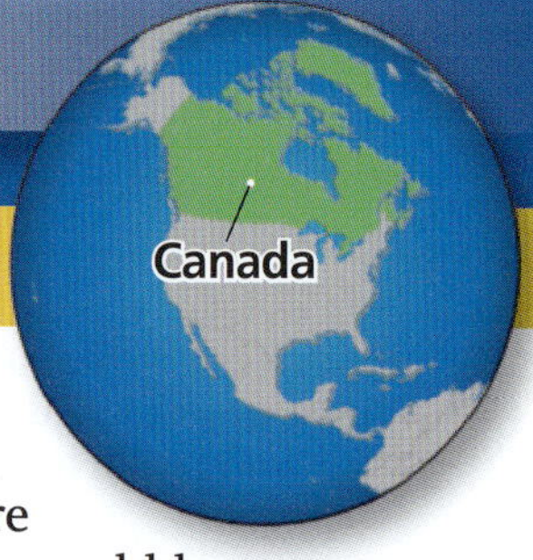

Canada today is a multicultural society. We have two official languages, English and French, but many other languages are spoken too. Immigrants from all over the world have come to live here. Each community brings its own customs and traditions, and as a result daily life can be very interesting!

For example, I'm from a Canadian Inuit family in north-west Canada and my boyfriend is French-Canadian from Quebec, in the east. I haven't met my boyfriend's family yet. I've spoken to his parents by phone – but my French is terrible and their English isn't great either. We met at university and started going out together last year. That's a normal way for a lot of Canadians to get together but my friend, Gurindah, thinks it's amazing. Her parents are from India and they have a different way of doing things. They don't let her choose her own boyfriends – they ask an Indian astrologer to help them select boys from their community. The astrologer has a website which lots of parents in India use too. But Gurindah says the boys must be from Canada!

We live in Vancouver, and there's a big Chinese community here. Two of my classmates were born in Hong Kong. Neither of them has a Chinese girlfriend and their parents are upset about that, I think. They want to organise a wedding in the traditional Chinese way. That means the parents choose the bride, but I think my friends prefer the Canadian system!

3 Read the text again and answer the questions.

1 How did the writer meet her boyfriend?
2 How does her friend, Gurindah, meet boyfriends?
3 How are Canadian marriages different from traditional Chinese marriages?

4 Find words in the text which match the definitions.

1 A person who goes to live in a different country.
2 Things which people do as part of their cultural traditions.
3 People who 'read' the stars and write horoscopes.
4 A woman who is getting married.

Listening

5 5.9 **Listen to a radio chat show for young people. Where is Ravi's girlfriend from?**

6 5.9 **Listen again. Choose the correct option (a, b or c).**

1 What is Ravi's background?
   a He's Polish.
   b He's Indian.
   c He's Canadian.
2 Why doesn't his girlfriend want to go anywhere with him?
   a She's frightened.
   b She's angry.
   c She's embarrassed.
3 Who went back to Italy?
   a Sofia.
   b Sofia's family.
   c Nobody.
4 What happened to Sofia and her boyfriend?
   a They broke up.
   b They got married.
   c They stayed together.
5 What does Sofia say about her parents?
   a They like her boyfriend.
   b It isn't easy for them.
   c They're still angry.

History and English

Social networking

1 Work in pairs. Answer the questions below, then compare your answers.

1 When did online social networking begin?
2 What were the first social networking websites?
3 How old do you have to be to join *Facebook* or *Bebo*?
4 What can you do on social networking sites?

2 Read about online social networking and check your answers.

Do you belong to a social networking site? Did your parents have a homepage when they were teenagers? Probably not, because online social networking began less than 20 years ago. Some of the earliest online communities were *theGlobe.com, Geocities* and *Tripod*. *TheGlobe.com* (1994) and *Tripod* (1995) were both started by students who used chat rooms at university. Chat rooms were places where you could 'talk' online. Personal homepages were also becoming popular, but people had to make their pages themselves. When the concepts of the chat room and the homepage were combined, social networking 'exploded' in popularity. By 2006, 55 per cent of teenagers in the USA had online profiles. *MySpace, Bebo* and *Facebook* are now the biggest global networks, although they are not open to children under 13. A typical social networking site lets you upload photos, videos and music as well as chatting. There are many other networks in different countries and different languages, including sites which are for special interests. *Flickr*, for example, is a photography site and *Gen.com* is for people who are researching their family trees.

There are always different opinions about new cultural fashions – television, video games, mobile phones. Some people think they are bad, others think they are good. Parents, in particular, sometimes don't understand online social networking and worry about the contacts that their children make. On the other hand, teenagers know that being online is a great way to keep in touch with friends and to find out what's going on. People like belonging to groups – family, friends, sports clubs, etc. Today's technology lets us do this in new ways.

3 Work in pairs. Why do you think social networking sites are so popular? Use ideas from the text and your own ideas.

Project

You have to be 13 to join most social networking sites. What other things have age limits in your country? Work in pairs and make a poster.

TRUE STORY

Michael Wesch

1 Read the article and answer the questions.

1 A **cultural anthropologist** studies things about …
   - a living people, such as their beliefs and relationships.
   - b societies from the past, such as their bones and the tools they used.

2 If you **make up with** someone you have **fallen out with**, you …
   - a stop being friends.
   - b become friends again.

3 If you **connect people**, you …
   - a keep them apart.
   - b join them together.

4 Someone who is **lonely** has no company …
   - a but is perfectly happy.
   - b and is unhappy about it.

Michael Wesch, who was born in 1975, is a **cultural anthropologist** and an assistant professor at Kansas State University. Between 1999 and 2003, he went to the rainforest of Papua New Guinea, where he studied the local people. He found that they understood themselves and their relationships with each other, better than most of us. For example, the local people believe that their health depends on how well they get on with others. When they are ill, they try to **make up with** anyone they have **fallen out with**.

These days, Wesch is interested in the relationships which **connect** people who communicate through sites like YouTube and Facebook. He thinks that the internet can help us to become happier, but we must learn to use it properly. We like to think of ourselves as modern and independent, but there is a danger that we might begin to feel **lonely**.

The world is getting smaller and there are fewer places left to discover, so the work Wesch and people like him are doing is becoming more important. The internet and the human mind need careful exploration.

Millions of people have seen Wesch's videos on YouTube.

Wesch has won many awards for his teaching and his videos.

In 2009 Michael Wesch was named as an Emerging Explorer by National Geographic.

2 Which statements are true according to the text?

1 Wesch lived in the Papua New Guinea rainforest for four years.
2 He studied the local people of Kansas.
3 The people of Papua New Guinea understand each other very well.
4 They believe that bad relationships can cause illness.
5 Wesch thinks that an internet relationship is the same as a real one.
6 These days, explorers do not have to travel in order to make important discoveries.

3 Discuss one or more of the following questions with a partner.

- Do you think studying other societies helps us understand our own?
- Is it better or worse to live in a society without computers and the internet?
- Can using computers make us lonely?

Science & technology 6

> Grammar

Learn about the first conditional, predictions with *will/won't, may* and *might*, and *going to* for plans and intentions.

> Vocabulary

Learn words for technology and science subjects. Work with verbs and prepositions, and phrasal verbs.

> Skills

Read about the first episode of *Star Trek*, and American sci-fi.

Listen to students' plans for the future, and to a discussion about sci-fi books and films.

Write instructions.

> Communicate

Make offers and requests, and accept help.

1 Look at the photo and choose the best caption (a, b or c).

- a This high-tech earpiece can send and receive messages and photos.
- b This microchip is smaller than a postage stamp, but it can store more information than 12 CDs.
- c Technologists have designed a small, hand-held screen which is also a webcam and video camera.

2 6.1 **Listen to Lauren and Aneta. They have to guess gadgets with five questions. What are the three gadgets? Find them in the vocabulary box.**

a digital book · a DVD · an earpiece · a flat screen TV · a GPS · a laptop · a memory stick · a microchip · a mobile phone · an MP3 player · a modem · a palmtop · a webcam

3 Work in pairs and prepare a questionnaire to find out who knows the most about technology in your class. Write five questions about gadgets. Use the verbs in the box below or your own ideas.

e.g. Do you know how to copy files on a computer?

copy · download · send · store · take · upload · use

4 Work with a new partner. Ask and answer your questions.

6A Back to the future

The Daily News

Sept 8, 1966

Last night's TV: Star Trek

The first episode of a new science-fiction series was shown on NBC last night. *Star Trek* is about a spacecraft which travels faster than the speed of light. The show is based on three ideas about the 22nd century. First, we'll find other life forms in our galaxy. Second, we won't fight with these aliens. And third, we'll have high-tech gadgets which will make amazing things possible.

Let's think about these predictions. If we find life forms on other planets, will they be intelligent? I hope so. But we human beings might not be friendly – I don't think we'll believe in the idea of peace two hundred years from now. But this is science fiction, so we can be optimistic! And *Star Trek*'s idea of life in the future is a lot of fun. For example, we'll be able to talk to each other with hand-held 'communicators'. And we'll be able to have conversations with people who are on different planets, on a giant TV screen. You won't have to use a pen and paper to write, because you'll have an electronic notepad. And if you get ill, the doctor won't have to examine you – a machine will 'read' your body. The strangest machine consists of a 'teleport' machine which will transport people to a different place in a second!

The ideas are very entertaining, and in my opinion, there's only one problem with *Star Trek*: the acting. The TV company will have to get better actors. If they do that, the show might be a success. If they don't, *Star Trek* won't last for more than one series. Of course, my prediction may be wrong. I can't see into the future!

Speaking

1 Look at the photo. Which film or TV series are these characters from? How many science-fiction films and TV series can you name? Tell your partner about the ones that you like best.

Reading and listening

2 Read the newspaper article quickly and answer the questions.

1 When was the article written?
2 What is it about?
3 What does the journalist predict?

3 6.2 **Read and listen to the article. Which Star Trek gadgets exist today? What do we call them?**

Grammar: first conditional

4 Complete the table with the words in the box.

get find will won't

condition	result
If you .... ill,	a machine will read your body.
If the acting doesn't improve,	Star Trek .... last for more than one series.
If we .... life forms,	.... they be intelligent?

See Grammar Explorer: Page 124

The future form of *can* is *will be able to*. The future form of *must* is *will have to*.

5 Choose the correct option.

1 We **don't** / **won't** need to buy books if digital books **become** / **will become** popular.

2 If you **go** / **will go** online, you **find** / **will find** the information you want.

3 **Can** / **Will** you be able to email me if you **don't** / **won't** take your computer?

4 If we **want** / **will want** to see them to see us on the computer, we **have to** / **will have to** get a webcam.

5 How **do** / **will** you contact me if you **haven't got** / **won't have** a mobile?

6 Complete the sentences with the verbs. Remember to use the present simple after *if*.

1 If Sally .... (**not / phone**), we .... (**not / know**) where she is.

2 .... it .... (**be**) quicker if she .... (**send**) a text message?

3 Andy .... (**not / get lost**) if he .... (**use**) the GPS.

4 I think my mum .... (**buy**) me an MP3 player if I .... (**pass**) my exams.

5 .... I .... (**can save**) my new settings if I .... (**change**) them?

Grammar: predicting

7 Match the sentences (1–5) with the meanings (a–c).

1 We will find other life forms.

2 We might find other life forms.

3 We won't find other life forms.

4 If other life forms exist, we will find them.

5 We may find other life forms.

a The prediction is not 100 per cent sure.

b The prediction is 100 per cent sure.

c The prediction depends on a condition.

See Grammar Explorer: Page 124

May and *might* have the same form for *I, you, he, she, it, we* and *they*.

8 Read the text again and find predictions to match each meaning (a–c) in Exercise 7. Compare with your partner.

9 Complete the predictions. Use *will, won't, may* or *might* depending on your opinion. Compare with your partner.

1 Faster-than-light travel .... possible. (**be**)

2 We .... life on other planets. (**find**)

3 We .... teleporters instead of cars. (**use**)

4 We .... on space stations in the Earth's orbit. (**can / live**)

Speaking

10 Work in pairs. Write at least two questions for each picture.

e.g. *Do you think we'll find alien life forms?*
What do you think they will look like?

an alien

a jetpack

a space city

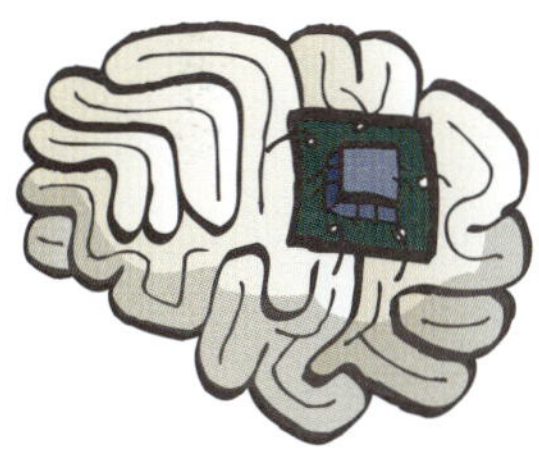
a brain

11 Work with a new partner. Ask and answer your questions from exercise 10.

e.g. A: *What do you think aliens will look like?*

B: *I think they'll have ... / I don't think they'll be ... / They might have...*

We use *I (don't) think ...* + *will* to express opinions.
We don't use *I think* + *won't....*

Working with words: verb + preposition

12 Look at the examples. Then read the text again and find verbs with the prepositions *on, in, to* and *for*.

Let's think about these predictions.

It consists of a 'teleport'.

See working with words: Page 106

Fast finishers

How quickly can you complete the words? They are all related to technology.

ear............	micro............
hand-............	note............
high-............	web............
lap............	

6B Science fact or fiction?

Science fact or fiction?

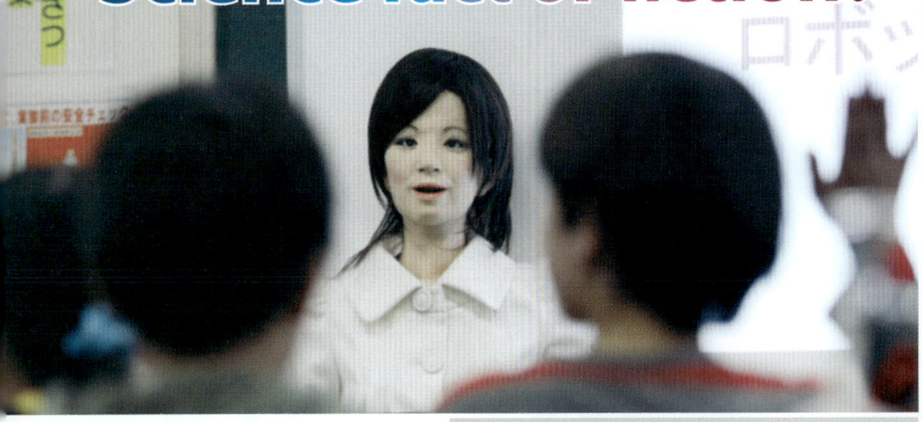

1 A team of engineers, computer scientists and physicians is working on a 'mind-reading' system. They have put a microchip into a man's brain. The microchip is connected to a computer. The man can switch on his email just by thinking about it. He can also turn up the volume of his TV. Now the team is going to make a smaller, wireless version of the system, which is called BrainGate.

2 Japanese schoolchildren love their robot teacher, Saya. She can speak, smile and tell students off. The Japanese government is going to invest millions of dollars in robot research and says it's going to put a robot in every Japanese home by 2015. However, psychologists predict that robot teachers won't take over from humans, because they will never be able to inspire their students.

3 British geneticists are going to vaccinate all school children with a 'smart gene'. The team of university scientists has identified the gene for intelligence on human DNA. Now they are going to put this gene into children under the age of twelve. Professor R. Ubbish says the vaccination won't work on adolescents or on children who don't like science.

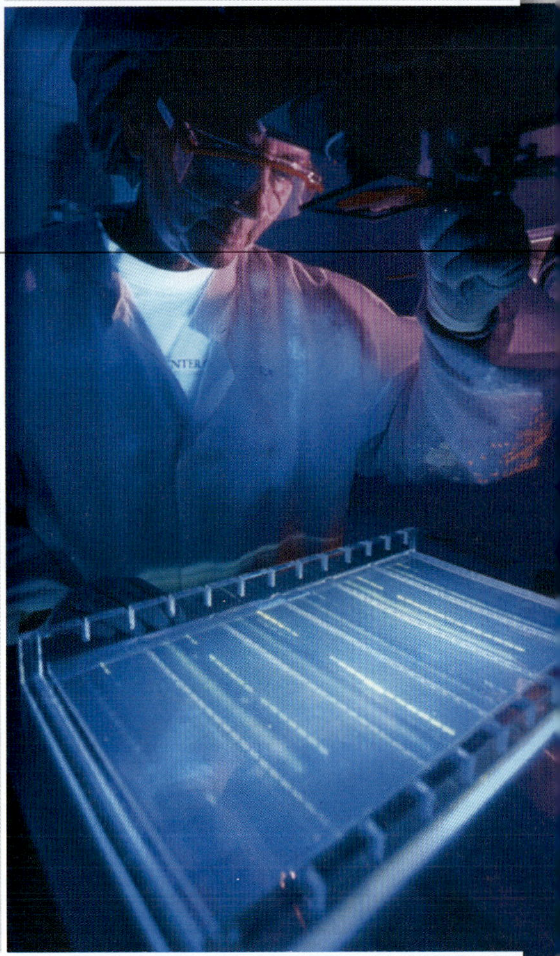

4 Biologists are going to study the effects of space travel on microscopic life forms. They want to find out if it's possible to survive for long periods in space. The micro-organisms are on an unmanned spacecraft which set off for Mars in 2009. It will land there, pick up some Martian soil and then come back to Earth. A team of geologists is going to analyse the soil. If everything goes well, the spacecraft will get back to Earth in two year's time.

Speaking

1 **Work in pairs. Discuss the questions (1–5) using words from the vocabulary box.**

astronomy	biochemistry	bio-technology	botany
chemistry	ecology	genetics	geography
geology	physics	psychology	zoology

1 Which science subjects do you study at school?
2 Which subjects are the most difficult?
3 Which subjects are the most interesting?
4 Which sciences help us understand our world?
5 Which sciences will help us to improve our lives in the future?

Reading and listening

2 6.3 **Read and listen to the text. Do you think the stories are true or false?**

3 STUDY SKILLS **Read the text again and look at the words in red. Are they nouns, verbs or adjectives?**

4 **Read the sentences in story 1 with the red words. Then choose the correct meanings.**

physicians

a things which scientists use

b people who work in an area of science

wireless

a without wires

b made of wire

5 **Work in pairs. Guess the meanings of the words in red in the other stories.**

Working with words: phrasal verbs

6 **Find these verbs in stories 1 and 4. Choose the correct meanings.**

turn up the volume = **a** increase **b** decrease

come back to Earth = **a** leave **b** return

See Working with words: Page 106

Grammar: *going to* for plans and intentions

7 **Look at the example. Then match them with the situations (1–5).**

The team is going to make a smaller, wireless version.

See Grammar Explorer: Page 124

8 **Complete the plans (a–e). Then match them with the situations (1–5).**

a Scientists .... the temperature of the ice. (**measure**)

b It .... the medicine next year. (**sell**)

c They .... here next year. (**come back**)

d Astronomers .... signals in outer space. (**look for**)

e The government .... more universities. (**build**)

1 A new telescope started working today.

2 The Arctic ice gives us information about climate change.

3 A drug company has developed a new cure for flu.

4 Lots of students want to study for a degree.

5 The scientists didn't **have time to** explore all the forest.

9 **Work in pairs. Read the comments from school students. What do you think they are going to or not going to do? Write sentences using the verbs in brackets.**

1 I'm good at biology at school. (**She / be**)

2 Chemistry is my favourite subject. (**He / work**)

3 Everyone in my family is a scientist. (**He / study**)

4 I finish school this year. (**She / look for**)

5 I'm doing French and Spanish at school. (**He / visit**)

Listening

10 6.4 **Listen to three students talking about their plans for the future. Match the sentences (a–d) with the students (1–3). There is one extra sentence.**

a He/She is going to do geology at university.

b He/she wants to be a zoologist.

c He/She is going to live abroad.

d He/She isn't going to follow the family tradition.

11 6.4 **Listen again. Complete the sentences.**

1 Student 1 knows all about ....

2 Student 2 isn't interested in ....

3 Student 3 is good at ....

Speaking

12 **Write questions with the words below and *going to*. Think about your own answers. Then work in pairs, and ask and answer the questions. Ask follow up questions.**

1 What / do / this afternoon?

2 What / watch / on TV tonight?

3 Who / get together with / this weekend?

4 Where go / in the next holidays?

5 What / do / on your next birthday?

Study skills

Difficult words

1 Decide if the word is a noun, a verb, an adjective, an adverb, etc..

2 Read the sentence carefully. Look at the words before and after the difficult word. What words can you use instead of this difficult word?

3 If you can't understand the sentence without understanding the word, use a dictionary.

6C How can I help you?

Reading and listening

1 6.5 **Read and listen to the dialogue. What does Lauren want to buy? Does she decide to buy one?**

2 **Read the dialogue again. Lauren asks for help three times. What does she say? Which expression is more formal?**

Assistant: How can I help you?
Lauren: I'd like to look at some mobile phones, please.
Assistant: If you follow me, I'll show you our selection.
Lauren: Thank you very much.
Assistant: These models are all very popular at the moment.
Lauren: I really like this one. It doesn't look like a phone! Can you explain how it works?
Assistant: Yes, of course! You switch it on here …
Lauren: Oh, yes … Aneta, can you hold my bag for me?
Aneta: Sure.
Lauren: Great, thanks. OK, has this phone got an MP3 player and a camera?
Assistant: Yes, it has. I'll put in a battery, just a moment.
Aneta: Lauren, have you seen the price? It's expensive.
Lauren: I know. I'll have to check with my mum. I don't think she'll let me spend that.
Assistant: Well, with this model you can download GPS and large files, and send emails.
Lauren: Hmm … I don't think I'll need all that.
Assistant: Shall I find some cheaper models?
Lauren: Yes, please. Could you show me something more basic?
Assistant: That's no problem. I'll just put this back in the box … Now, what about these?
Lauren: Oh, I like this one.
Aneta: Yeah, me too. It's just like mine!
Lauren: OK! I'll take it!

3 **Look at the *Useful expressions*. Who uses the expressions, the customer or the assistant?**

USEFUL EXPRESSIONS

How can I help you?
I'd like to look at some mobile phones, please.
I'll show you our selection.
Thank you very much.
Can you explain how it works?
Yes, of course.
Shall I find some cheaper models?
Yes, please.
Could you show me something more basic?
I'll take it!

4 6.6 **Listen and check your answers to Exercise 3. Then listen again and repeat.**

5 **Choose the correct option (a, b or c) for each situation.**

1 You are in a shop. You want to ask the shop assistant for help. What do you say?
  - **a** I'll help you.
  - **b** Can I help you?
  - **c** Could you help me?

2 The shop assistant offers to show you some cameras. What does he say?
  - **a** Can you show me this camera?
  - **b** I'll show you our cameras.
  - **c** How can I help you?

3 You want the shop assistant to show you a phone. What do you say?
  - **a** Could I show you this phone?
  - **b** Shall I show you a different model?
  - **c** I'd like to see this phone, please.

4 The shop assistant offers to show you how a camera works. How do you respond?
  - **a** I'll take it!
  - **b** Thank you very much.
  - **c** Yes, of course!

Speaking

6 **Work in pairs. For each situation, offer or request help, and respond. Take turns.**

1 carry / bags

2 put in / paper

3 fix / bike

4 connect / webcam

Pronunciation: connected speech

7 6.7 **Listen to the sentences. Notice how the underlined words are linked.**

1 Here are the headphones. Put them on.
2 I'd like to look at it.
3 Switch it on.
4 Put it in the printer.
5 Turn up the volume.

Writing: giving instructions

1 **Read the emails. What does Jack want? Does Aneta help?**

2 **Find examples of *so that* and *in order to* in the email. Then complete the sentences below with *so that* or *in order to*.**

1 I bought a DVD player .... we can watch films at home.
2 Aneta bought an MP3 player .... listen to music.
3 We installed Skype .... we can make free phone calls.
4 My dad wants a GPS .... plan a driving holiday this year.

See Grammar Explorer: Page 125

3 **Rewrite the sentences in Exercise 2 with the other expression.**

4 **Write a message to your partner asking for help. Reply to your partner's message and give instructions. You can use the ideas in the box or your own ideas.**

> download photos from a camera onto a computer
> put phone numbers into a phone memory
> record a TV programme

Aneta,
Can you explain how to put music files on my MP3 player? Could you come round tonight?

See you later!
Jack

Hi Jack,
Sorry – I'd love to help, but we're going to my grandparents' tonight. Shall I come round tomorrow? If you want to try it by yourself, this is what you do:
1 Download the songs that you want onto your computer.
2 Save the songs in a folder so that they are easy to find.
3 Plug in your USB cable in order to connect your MP3 player to the computer.
4 Click open 'My computer' so that you can open your MP3 player.
5 Drag your music files onto your MP3 player.

I'll call you later!
Aneta

6D American sci-fi

Reading

1 **Look at the photos. Which of these things can you see?**

aliens planets machines
the moon robots UFOs

2 6.8 **Listen and read about American sci-fi. How many American authors can you find?**

Culture

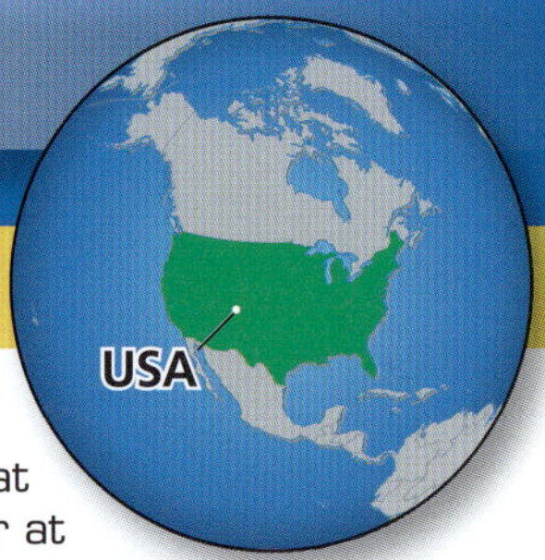

Science fiction – or sci-fi – is a different way of looking at the world. It became popular at a time when electricity, machines and new forms of transport were changing people's lives. European writers like Jules Verne and H.G. Wells wrote new stories for the new times – science fiction.

In the early 20th century, sci-fi stories in magazines and comics sold millions of copies in the USA. Books by American writers like Ray Bradbury, Robert A. Heinlein, Ursula K. Le Guin and Philip K. Dick are translated into almost every language in the world.

Some writers, such as Robert A Heinlein, focused on the kind of future that technology might bring. Sometimes, that future seemed too incredible. Heinlein's first book was rejected by some publishers. They said that 'to reach the moon' wasn't believable!

Other authors, such as Ursula K. Le Guin, wrote about culture and identity in the future. Le Guin was born in 1929, and wrote her first story when she was eleven years old. Her stories are often about contact between alien worlds in a way that teaches us something about our own human culture and society.

Both Heinlein and Le Guin influenced other writers, but neither of them had the impact on American films that Philip K. Dick had. *Blade Runner*, *Total Recall* and *Minority Report* are just three of the films which were adapted from Philip K. Dick's stories. Most of his stories are about space and time, parallel worlds and genetic engineering. He describes a future that is cruel, dangerous and frightening. Perfect for Hollywood movies!

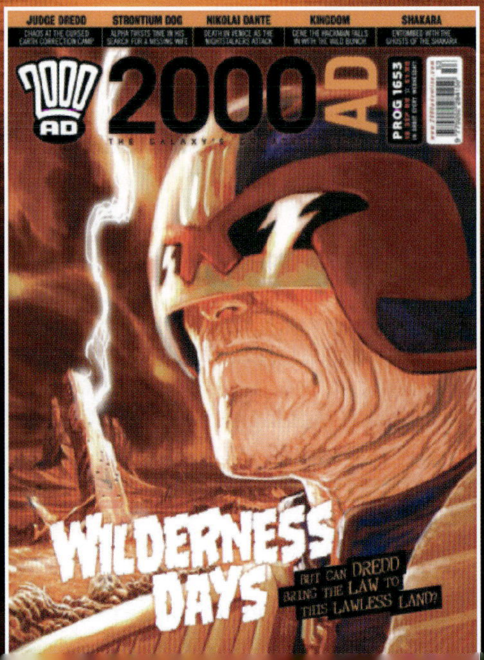

3 **Read the text again and answer the questions.**

1 When did science-fiction writing become popular?
2 Where was science fiction first published?
3 Why did Robert A Heinlein have difficulty getting his first book published?
4 Which author's books help us to understand our society?
5 Which author's stories were often made into films?

4 **Work in pairs. Find these words in the text and try to guess their meaning. Then use them to complete the sentences below.**

way incredible reach impact

1 The spacecraft set off last year and will .... Mars next year.
2 The experiment didn't work, so they will try a new .... of doing it.
3 The meteor made a huge .... when it hit the Earth.
4 Astronauts have walked on the Moon . I think that's ....

Listening

5 6.9 **Listen to two people talking about science fiction. Then choose the correct option (a, b or c).**

a They both think films are better than books.
b They agree that books are better than films.
c They can't agree which is better – films or books.

6 6.9 **Listen again. Complete the sentences with *man* or *woman*.**

1 The ....'s favourite actor is Tom Cruise.
2 The .... doesn't like Philip K. Dick's stories.
3 The ....'s favourite film is *E.T.*
4 The .... thinks the book *War of the Worlds* is old-fashioned.
5 The .... recommends the film *Minority Report*.

Physics and English

Telescopes

1 **What do we use to look at the planets in our solar system? Read about telescopes and find out how they work.**

Light and telescopes

How do we see things?

Light travels in straight lines. When light hits an object, it reflects off the object and comes back into our eyes. For example, light travels out from the sun in all directions. When the light reaches a planet, it is reflected back by the planet. From Earth, we see this light and so we see the image of the planet. The rest of space looks black because there are no planets to stop the light and reflect it back to us.

How do telescopes make things seem larger and closer?

Telescopes collect the straight lines of light (A) and change their direction. They do this with a lens (B). The lens bends the light so that it focuses to a point (C). This makes it easier to see, but the image is still very small. In order to see the image, we have to make it bigger. A second lens is used to do this (D). In this way, when the reflected light reaches our eyes (E), the objects seem larger and closer than they are.

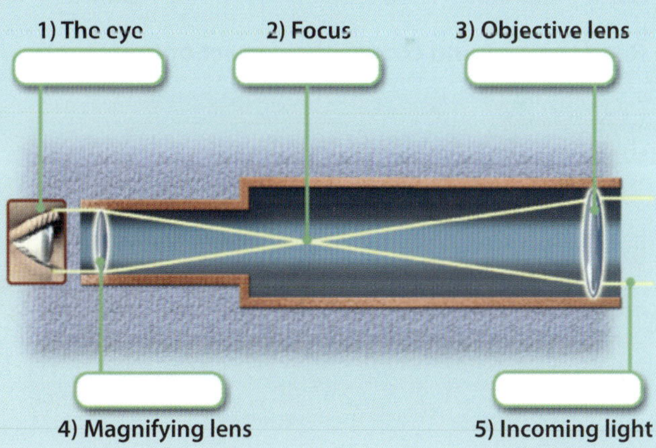

2 **Complete in the diagram to the letters (A–E) from the text.**

Project

What is your favourite science fiction film or story? Write a paragraph saying who directed/wrote it and what it is about. Then write a second paragraph saying why you like this film or story.

Consolidation Units 5 and 6

Gapped text

Choosing the correct word form

- Read the whole text quickly, once.
- Look at the gapped sentences again. Try to predict the missing words. Decide what kind of words they are.
- Look at the options for each gap. Choose the option that matches the grammar or logic of the gapped sentence.

Important! Be careful with easily confused words.

1 Read the sentences. What do you think the missing word is – a noun, a verb or an adjective?

1 I love my sister. She's funny and ....
2 My dad and I .... really well. We like the same things.
3 There are three .... in my family – two boys and a girl.

2 Read the sentences in Exercise 1 again and choose words that can go in each gap.

3 Look at the options for each gap in Exercise 1. Are any of the words that you chose here? Choose the correct answers.

1	a	kind	b	kinder	c	kindest
2	a	fight	b	take after	c	get on
3	a	children	b	child	c	brothers

4 Read the text and choose the correct option (a–c).

Dear Jenny,

Thanks for sending the photos of your holidays. You're a (1) .... photographer than me! The last time I (2) .... a photo, I chopped off everyone's heads! China looks amazing! (3) .... the people nice? Everyone looks friendly. When did you get back? Let's meet up at the weekend – school (4) .... again on Monday!

David

1	a	good	b	better	c	the best
2	a	was taking	b	take	c	took
3	a	Was	b	Did	c	Were
4	a	starts	b	was starting	c	start

Listening

Identifying the main idea

- Read the task instruction and the options.
- Identify the overall topic.
- For matching questions, read the questions again and underline the key words.
- For multiple-choice questions, try to predict words you will hear.
- The first time you listen, choose the correct answer. The second time, check your answers.

Important! Be careful with words that have similar meanings.

1 Read the task instruction and options. Find the overall topic and the key words.

You will hear three people talk about their favourite gadgets. Match the statements (a–d) with each speaker (1–3). There is one extra statement.

a It's really useful when I'm travelling.
b I like it because I can listen to music everywhere.
c It makes it easy for me to stay in touch with my parents.
d It's easy to use and the picture is great.

2 Read the task instruction and options. Write words you think you will hear for each option.

You will hear someone talk about their favourite gadget. What is the gadget?

a a webcam
b a memory stick
c a mobile phone

3 6.10 **Now listen and do the task in Exercise 1.**

4 6.11 **You will hear someone talk about a birthday present. What is the present? Choose the correct option (a–c).**

a a laptop
b an MP3 player
c a GPS

Prepositions after verbs

Some verbs can be followed by prepositions: *consist of*, *believe in*. Some verbs are never followed by prepositions.

1 **Choose the correct option.**

1 Do you listen **the radio / to the radio** every day?
2 My friend apologised **me / to me** after our argument.
3 I usually phone **my grandparents / to my grandparents** on Sundays.
4 Can you explain **me / to me** how this phone works?
5 Will you call **me / to me** tonight, please? I'll be at home.
6 Read the sentences and discuss **them / about them**.

2 **Write the missing prepositions.**

1 Who are you talking ....?
2 What are you talking ....?
3 What kind of music do you listen ....?
4 What are you looking ....?
5 Who are you waiting ....?
6 Who are you going shopping ....?

Prepositions in time expressions

3 **Complete the sentences with *at* or *on*. Write – if the sentence is already correct.**

1 I'm going to visit my friend .... next month.
2 What are you doing .... five o' clock?
3 Where did you go .... last week?
4 Do you want to meet .... Saturday morning?
5 I don't like going out .... night.
6 We watched a great programme on TV .... last night.

Prepositions in phrasal verbs

4 **Match the prepositions with opposite meanings.**

back from in into on up

down forward off out out of to

5 **Complete the sentences with prepositions from Exercise 4.**

a

b

c

d

e

f

1 Where do you come ....?
2 What time did we set ....?
3 Can you fill .... this form, please?
4 I'm not making .... with him!
5 Calm .... It's not important.
6 I'll call you ....!

Prepositions that are easy to confuse

6 **Choose the correct option.**

1 Can you translate this **in / into** Spanish?
2 How many students are **in / into** your class?
3 I opened the door and the dog ran **in / into** the garden.
4 There are lots of animals **in / into** the park.
5 The book was made **in / into** a film.

7 **Which preposition can be used to complete all these sentences?**

1 Ben fell his .... bike.
2 We got .... the bus.
3 I took the picture .... the wall.
4 I took .... my coat.

Review Units 5 and 6

Vocabulary

1 Complete the description.

The man has (**1**) d............. h............. and a (**2**) t............. on his neck. He's wearing some (**3**) j............. – an (**4**) e............. and a gold (**5**) n............. .

1 mark per item: .../5 marks

2 Circle the correct adjectives.

1 My friends have gone on holiday. I'm **lonely / excited**.
2 I feel **anxious / annoyed** when I go to the dentists.
3 I was **pleased / upset** after I argued with my mum.
4 I feel **embarrassed / cheerful** on sunny days.
5 I was **disappointed / confident** when I got a D for my project.

1 mark per item: .../5 marks

3 Write the names of the objects.

1 ....
2 ....
3 ....
4 ....
5 ....

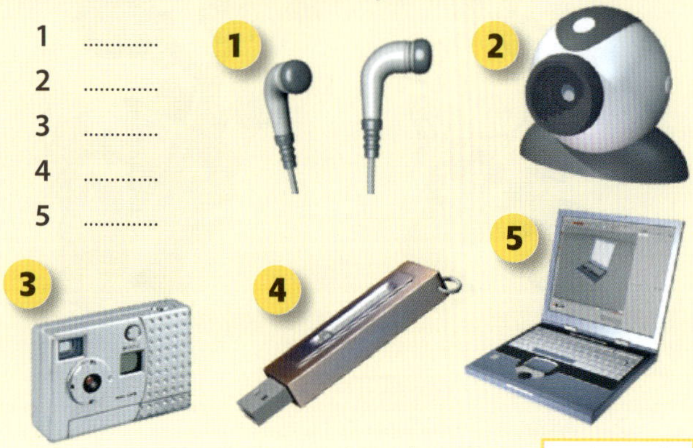

1 mark per item: .../5 marks

4 Write the science subjects.

1 The study of space and the planets: ....
2 The study of soil and rocks: ....
3 The study of animals: ....
4 The study of the brain and behaviour: ....
5 The study of DNA and genes: ....

1 mark per item: .../5 marks

5 Complete the sentences.

1 People who accept new ideas are ....-............. .
2 My brother's going .... with his friends tonight.
3 I don't believe .... Santa Claus.
4 Oh, I haven't got enough money to pay .... my bus ticket.
5 How did you find .... when my birthday is?

1 mark per item: .../5 marks

Grammar

6 Rewrite the sentences using the words in brackets.

1 We can't wear trainers at school. (**allowed**)
2 My mum makes me tidy my bedroom everyday. (**have to**)
3 I can't wear nail varnish. (**my parents / not let**)
4 Can you stay out after ten o'clock? (**allowed**)
5 Mobile phones are not allowed in class. (**must / use**)

1 mark per item: .../5 marks

7 Complete the sentences with *who*, *when*, *which* or *where*.

1 The rocket .... went to Mars has landed.
2 A person .... writes books is an author.
3 The time .... people sleep is the night.
4 The man .... wrote *I, Robot* was American.
5 The café .... we met was great.

1 mark per item: .../5 marks

8 Make first conditional sentences.

1 If you .... (**take**) your mobile, I .... (**call**) you.
2 My dad .... (**worry**) if I .... (**not / phone**) home soon.
3 If there .... (**be**) life on another planet, ... it .... (**be**) friendly?
4 If we .... (**not / use**) the GPS, we .... (**not / find**) the road.
5 .... Ben .... (**listen**) to me if I .... (**talk**) to him?

2 marks per item: .../10 marks

10 Complete the sentences with the correct form of *be able to* or *have to*.

1 I .... download files. (**can**)
2 We .... arrive on time. (**must**)
3 .... watch TV this evening? (**can I**)
4 We .... stay out late. (**can't**)
5 .... save this file? (**must I**)

1 mark per item: .../10 marks

Communicate

11 Choose the correct responses (a, b or c).

1 This phone seems very complicated.
  a Thank you very much.
  b Shall I find a simpler model?
  c How can I help you?

2 Do you want to borrow my camera?
  a Yes, of course.
  b I'd like to look at some cameras.
  c Thanks. Can you explain how it works?

3 This memory stick costs €5.
  a Shall I find some cheaper models?
  b I'll take it.
  c Yes, please.

4 How can I help you?
  a I'll show you our selection.
  b I'd like to look at some laptops.
  c Shall I show you how it works?

5 Can you switch the printer on?
  a Yes, please.
  b Yes, of course.
  c I'd like to switch the printer on.

2 marks per item: .../10 marks

12 Do the pairs of words sound the same or different?

1	pair	pear
2	their	there
3	cheer	chair
4	hair	here
5	where	were

2 marks per item: .../10 marks

13 Complete the sentences with *so that* or *in order to*.

1 I borrowed a mobile .... make a phone call.
2 I'm going to study medicine .... I can become a doctor.
3 We went on the Internet .... we could find the information.
4 My friend lent me his bike .... I didn't have walk to school.
5 We got broadband .... have a faster connection.

2 marks per item: .../10 marks

14 Complete the dialogue with the expressions.

Cheer up. Let's go shopping!
I can't believe that!
It's not the end of the world.
Tell me all about it.
What's wrong?

Lisa: (**1**) ....
Jo: I'm worried about my IT test results.
Lisa: (**2**) ....
Jo: I did badly in my test and my dad always gets angry when I get bad marks.
Lisa: (**3**) .... Isn't he easy-going?
Jo: Not really. This is a disaster!
Lisa: (**4**) ....
Jo: I know. But you don't know my dad.
Lisa: (**5**) ....

2 marks per item: .../10 marks

15 Complete the text with these words.

after all both both of going to neither that them where will

There are five people in my family. I've got two sisters. I take (**1**) .... my dad. (**2**) .... us are tall and dark. (**3**) .... of my sisters is dark, in fact they are very blond. My parents are (**4**) .... scientists and we (**5**) .... like sci-fi. Next month, we're (**6**) .... take part in a *Star Trek* convention. It's a big party (**7**) .... *Star Trek* fans meet. My sisters love dressing up. Both of (**8**) .... are going to the convention as aliens (**9**) .... have invaded Earth! I think we (**10**) .... have a great time.

1 mark per item: .../10 marks

Total: .../100

I can...

I can talk about problems.
I can make offers and requests.
I can accept help.

PROJECT

Predicting the future

What is going to happen?

Most of us want to know about what will happen in the future. Here are a few things to think about ...

Crime | Accommodation | Space Exploration | The Environment | Medicine | Social Life

1 Read the predictions and match them to the headings above.

1 ....

Many people think that we will need to travel to other planets to look for more resources. But this is not going to happen in the near future. We may have to wait hundreds, or thousands of years.

2 ....

Experts say that we will stop meeting in groups. Many of us will only have contact with the outside world through our computers or hand-held devices.

3 ....

Most predictions add up to one thing: if we don't do something quickly, the planet will probably be destroyed. It is impossible to say exactly when his might happen but some people predict might happen in our lifetime.

4 ....

Most people are hopeful that we will discover cures for serious health problems. However, nobody knows how prepared we will be for the next terrible virus.

5 ....

This will certainly still exist in the future but it will probably be more sophisticated. Most offences will probably be computer-related, as we are going to do more of our financial dealings over the internet.

6 ....

With six billion people, the world is struggling to house everyone. As people move to the cities, houses will have to get smaller, and people will have much less space.

Computers | Transport | Education | Communication | Explorers | Work | Entertainment

2 With a partner, discuss your predictions for the headings above. Use some of the following phrases:

If ... will ...

Humans/We/People will/might/won't ...

... will ...

... might/may ...

... will probably ...

... in the near future ...

Experts say that ...

It is impossible to say ...

... is/are hopeful that ...

Nobody knows ...

... will have to ...

Project

Write about your predictions for the future.

- Choose 6 headings from Exercises 1 and 2 (or choose your own)
- Write about what you think *will / is going to* happen
- You can also write about things that *might/may* happen and use the first conditional
- Try to find interesting pictures showing the situation now or in the future (or draw your own)

NATIONAL GEOGRAPHIC

7 Citizens

> Grammar

Learn about reporting verbs: *ask, tell, order, want and warn,* reported requests and orders, and indirect questions.

> Vocabulary

Learn words for cities and towns, and crime. Work with words that are easy to confuse, and irregular nouns.

> Skills

Read witness statements, read about the European Youth Parliament, and a Maori tradition in New Zealand.

Listen to a conversation at a forum, and to a Maori girl.

Write a note with personal news.

> Communicate

Give and take messages.

1 **Where do you think the photo was taken? Why?**

2 7.1 **Listen to three people talking about where they live. Answer the questions for each person.**

1 Do they live in the city or the country?

2 Do they like living there?

3 **Work in groups of four. Which is better – living in the city or in the country? Use words from the vocabulary box and these expressions.**

There are more … / There aren't as many … / It isn't as … / It's less … in the city/country.

a city centre **art galleries** **graffiti** **ice rinks** **leisure centre** **litter** **office blocks** **public transport** **shopping centres** **skate parks** **sports stadiums** **youth centres**

7A Gangs

Speaking

1 **Work in pairs. Can you name the films in the photos? Match the films with the correct information.**

Film	Character	Gang
8 Mile Grease West Side Story	Bernado Danny Maria Rabbit Sandy Tony	Leaders of the Free World The Jets The Pink Ladies The Sharks The T-Birds

2 **Look at the words in the box. Put them into two groups: *people* and *crimes*.**

a burglary   a criminal   a detective   fighting
a gang   a mugging   the police   a robbery
shoplifting   a thief   vandalism   a victim   a witness

Reading and listening

3 **Three people saw a crime. Read their witness statements quickly and decide what the crime was. Choose one of the options.**

a Fighting.
b Shoplifting.
c Vandalism.

The customer

It was about ten o'clock. I was going home when my husband phoned and reminded me to rent some DVDs for the weekend. There was a group of teenagers in the street. They were all watching a dark-haired boy who was going into the DVD shop. The tallest boy told him to hurry up, I think. I went into the shop and I went to the shelf where the action movies are. After a few minutes, I heard a lot of shouting. A woman ordered somebody to raise their hands! It was very dramatic – just like in a film!

The shop assistant

It was about five minutes before closing time. There were only two customers: a smartly-dressed woman and a teenage boy. The boy asked me to help him. He was looking for *Alien*. He wanted me to find it for him. I had to leave my desk and go into the back of the shop. I didn't really see what happened, but the shop manager suddenly came out of her office. She told me to lock the front door and to call the police. She was holding the boy by the arm. She warned him not to move. The police arrived a few minutes later.

The shop manager

I was watching the last two people in the shop. There was a boy who looked nervous and anxious. He said something to my assistant and my assistant left the counter. Then the boy went behind the counter, picked up some DVDs and put them inside his jacket. I ran out of my office and ordered the boy to open his jacket. He didn't, but he put his hand in his pocket. I felt a bit worried at that point, so I asked my assistant to follow our emergency procedure.

4 7.2 **Read and listen to the witness statements. Who do you think said these things? Match the comments (1–6) to the people (a, b, c or d).**

1 'Can you help me?'
2 'Could you find *Alien*, please?'
3 'Don't forget to rent some DVDs.'
4 'Don't move!'
5 'Hurry up!'
6 'Unzip your jacket right now!'

a The dark-haired boy.
b The tallest boy.
c The customer's husband.
d The shop manager.

Grammar: reporting verbs

5 **Read the witness statements again. Then complete the chart.**

a My husband	....	me	to rent some DVDs.
b The tallest boy	....	him	to hurry up.
c The boy	....	me	to help him.
d He	....	me	to find it.
e She	....	him	not to move
f I	....	the boy	to open his jacket.

See Grammar Explorer: Page 125

We can use … someone to … with the verbs *ask*, *invite*, *order*, *remind*, *tell*, *want* and *warn*.

6 **Match the comments (1–6) in Exercise 4 with the sentences (a–f) in the table in Exercise 5.**

7 **Read the sentences (1–5) below. What did the people in red actually say? Choose the correct option (a or b).**

1 The gang leader invited the boy to join the gang.
  a 'Do you want to be in my gang?'
  b 'Don't forget to join my gang.'
2 The gang told him to steal the DVDs.
  a 'Can you steal some DVDs, please?'
  b 'Steal those DVDs.'
3 The gang leader warned the boy not to tell the police.
  a 'Don't tell the police.'
  b 'Do you want to tell the police?'
4 The boy wanted the gang to like him.
  a 'Can I be in your gang?'
  b 'Don't talk to me.'
5 The policewoman asked the witness to give a statement.
  a 'Give a statement now.'
  b 'Can you give a statement, please?'

8 **Report a policewoman's words with the verbs.**

e.g. 'Go home, everybody!' (**tell / everybody**)
She told everybody to go home.

1 'Please phone the police station.' (**ask / witnesses**)
2 'Don't join gangs.' (**warn / teenagers**)
3 'Keep calm!' (**order / the crowd**)
4 'Don't panic!' (**tell / victim**)
5 'Don't forget to write a report.' (**remind / the policeman**)

9 **Look at the notices (a–d) and complete the sentences (1–4).**

1 Sign .... warns people not to ....
2 Sign .... asks customers to .... for help.
3 Sign .... reminds people not to ....
4 Sign .... tells people to ....

Working with words: words that are easy to confuse

10 **Look at the examples. What's the difference in the way we use *say* and *tell*?**

say He said something to my assistant.
tell She told me to lock the front door.

See Working with words: Page 107

Fast finishers

What do you call someone who does these things?

breaks the law steals things
investigates crime sees a crime
is robbed

7B European youth

City people

Meet Albert Reverendo

1 It's July 2009, and Albert Reverendo, aged 16, of Girona, Spain is looking forward to the summer holidays. He'll be able to play water-polo with his team, and he might be able to do some acting, which is another one of his interests. But politics is also one of Albert's intrests, and this summer he's going to the European Youth Parliament (EYP) International Forum. It's in Girona this year.

Albert talks about the European Youth Parliament
The European Youth Parliament is a network for young people, aged from 16 to 22, who are interested in changing their world. It's a real opportunity to make a difference, instead of just sitting at home and complaining about things. The EYP actually has a representative in the European Parliament. There are committees on different subjects – immigration, climate change, and culture and education are the ones which interest me the most. At the Forum in Girona, I'll meet people from nearly all the countries in Europe, go to lots of parties, and I'll do it all in English!

2 **Albert says …**
'Come and join the European Youth Parliament and get involved in our project. I encourage you to be an active and responsible young citizen. It's not only about politics, it's also about developing yourself as a person, meeting some great people, and having great fun.'

Speaking

1 **Work in pairs. Which of these things are you interested in?**

art · going out with friends · music · making new friends · politics · people in other countries · sport · the environment

Reading and listening

2 **Read the texts (1–3) quickly. Then match each text with the descriptions (a–e). There are two extra descriptions.**

- a The writer is asking for information.
- b The writer is offering advice.
- c The writer is inviting someone to do something.
- d The writer is giving information.
- e The writer is offering help.

3 7.3 STUDY SKILLS **Read and listen to the texts. Find words in the texts with similar meanings to the words in the box.**

hobbies · meeting · organisation · chance · topics · take part in · enjoying yourself · pianist · play with

4 **What can you remember? Cover the texts. Then say if the sentences below are true or false.**

1. Albert's free-time activities are water-polo and playing the piano.
2. Primary-school pupils can take part in the Forum.
3. Albert will be able to practise English at the Forum.
4. The EYP is a group for people who are interested in politics.
5. Catarina is a delegate at the Forum.

3

Iberian Forum '09 Guestbook

Date 2 March
From Catarina Pires
Subject application

EUROPEAN YOUTH PARLIAMENT
PARLEMENT EUROPÉEN DES JEUNES

Hi!
Could anyone tell me how I apply to be a delegate at the Forum? Also, do you know what the dates of the Forum are?

Date 10 July
From Andris
Subject euro-concert

Hi there ... I'm attending the Forum and I'd like to sing at the concert. But ... I need a piano player to accompany me. Can you tell me if there are any participants who can join me?

Working with words: irregular nouns

5 Look at the examples. Do you know any more irregular nouns?

politics — Politics is an interesting subject.
the police — The police are at the scene.

See working with words: Page 107

Grammar: word order in indirect questions

6 Complete the questions from the text.

1 Could anyone tell me how .... to be a delegate?
2 Do you know what the dates of the Forum ....?
3 Can you tell me if .... any participants who can join me?

See Grammar Explorer: Page 125

7 Look at the example. Then rewrite the questions in Exercise 6 without the words in red.

e.g. Can you tell me what time it is?
What time is it?

8 Rewrite the questions as indirect questions.

1 What time does the Forum start?
2 How do I get to Girona from Paris?
3 Are there T-shirts in all sizes?

9 STUDY SKILLS Look at the groups of words. Which one is the odd one out?

1 laptop mobile phone
2 book programme show
3 half an hour a moment 30 minutes
4 enjoy yourself feel lonely have a great time
5 photo picture signature

Listening

10 7.4 Listen to two delegates at the Forum in Girona. Are the sentences true or false?

1 Yannis saw Tina's photo on the Forum website.
2 Yannis is having a great time at the Forum.
3 Tina's memory is full.
4 Tina's next session starts in 30 minutes.

Speaking

11 Work in pairs. Plan a party or a school festival. Make notes on time, place, number of people, activities, entry fee, etc.

12 Work with a new partner. Ask and answer questions about the events. Use polite questions.

A: *Can you tell me what your event is?*
B: *Yes. It's an end-of-term party.*

Study skills

Synonyms

1 Texts use similar words or synonyms to avoid repetition.
2 When you are answering questions about a text, listen and look for words which are similar to the words in the questions.
3 Write groups of similar words in your notebook.

7C Giving and taking messages

Reading and listening

1 7.5 **Read and listen to the dialogue. Are the sentences true or false?**

1 Aneta can't go to the picnic.
2 Jack's got a jacket for Lee.
3 Lee's going to take chocolate cookies to the picnic.

2 **Read the dialogue again. Find Jack's message. How does Lee's gran pass on Jack's message?**

Gran: Hello.
Jack: Hi. Can I speak to Lee, please?
Gran: Oh, Lee's gone shopping. This is his gran speaking.
Jack: Oh, hello. It's Jack. Could you give him a message, please?
Gran: With pleasure, Jack.
Jack: Can you tell him Aneta's going to the picnic tomorrow?
Gran: Yes, of course.
Jack: And remind him to take some biscuits and cake to the picnic. Oh, and can you ask him to lend me a jacket?
Gran: OK. I'll tell him.
Jack: Thank you very much.
Gran: You're welcome.

Later that day …

Gran: Hello, Lee.
Lee: Hi, Gran.
Gran: Your friend Jack phoned. He says Aneta's going to the picnic tomorrow.
Lee: Really? That's great!
Gran: And he says he wants to borrow a jacket from you.
Lee: That's OK. I've got two.
Gran: And he asked me to remind you to take some biscuits and cake.
Lee: Oh, no. I forgot to buy biscuits at the shops!
Gran: I'll make some chocolate cookies, then. Is that OK?
Lee: Yes, that's great! I'll do the washing up for you! Thanks, Gran.
Gran: Not at all. I'm always happy to help my grandson!

3 7.6 **Listen and repeat the *Useful expressions*. Focus on your intonation.**

USEFUL EXPRESSIONS

Could you give him a message, please?
With pleasure.
Can you tell him Aneta's coming to the picnic tomorrow?
Remind him to take some biscuits and cake.
Can you ask him to lend me a jacket?
I'll tell him.
You're welcome.
He says Aneta's going to the picnic tomorrow.
He says he wants to borrow a jacket from you.
He asked me to remind you to take some biscuits and cake.

4 7.7 **Listen to the messages (1–3) and choose the correct answers (a, b or c).**

1 What does Jack ask Lauren's mum to do?
 a Give a note to Lauren.
 b Remind Lauren to come to the picnic.
 c Remind Lauren to bring her camera.

2 Why does Lauren phone Aneta?
 a To apologise for not meeting her.
 b To invite her to lunch.
 c To change the time of their meeting.

3 What does Aneta want Lee to do?
 a Phone her back.
 b Finish their project.
 c Meet after school today.

5 **Match the questions (1–3) with the answers (a–d). There is one extra answer.**

1 Can you give Aneta a message, please?
2 What's the message?
3 Can you tell her to phone me back?

a Can you remind her to bring our project to school tomorrow?
b It's really important.
c Of course. I'll tell her to call you.
d With pleasure.

Speaking

6 **You are going to a party with your friend tomorrow. You leave a message with her/his dad. Write the message. You can use the phrases in the box to help you. Then, in pairs, take turns giving and taking your messages.**

Can you tell her/him ... ?
Remind her/him ... .
Can you ask her/him ... ?

Pronunciation: words ending in /p/ and /b/, /k/ and /g/, /f/ and /v/

7 7.8 **Listen and repeat the groups of words.**

1	cap	hip	hop	lip	shop	map
2	cab	rob	pub	rub	job	web
3	back	dock	lock	Dick	Jack	pick
4	bag	dog	log	dig	jag	pig
5	leaf	life	off	stuff	half	laugh
6	leave	live	of	five	have	drive

8 7.9 **Listen and repeat. Be careful with the final sound.**

1	cap	cab
2	back	bag
3	pick	pig
4	leaf	leave
5	off	of
6	half	have

Writing: personal news

1 **Read Lauren's note to her cousin, Erin, in Ireland. Which subjects does Lauren talk about?**

her boyfriend taking part in a competition
doing sport Aneta and Lee her family Jack

2 **Find these words and expressions in Lauren's note. Then choose the correct option.**

Actually Unfortunately By the way
Guess what? luckily Anyway

Hi Erin,

(**1**) **Guess what? / Anyway,** I took my driving test last week. (**2**) **Unfortunately, / Luckily,** I didn't pass. (**3**) **By the way, / Actually,** I was terrible! (**4**) **Anyway, / Unfortunately,** I can try again next month!

Love, Rosie

3 **Write a note to a friend giving them some personal news. Use some of the expressions from Exercise 2.**

Congratulations!

Hi Erin,

Congratulations! You've passed your driving test! (My dad told me!) That's great.

Sorry I haven't written for a while. I've been really busy with the hockey team and rowing club. Actually, I rowed in my first competition race last weekend. Unfortunately, we didn't win, but we didn't come last, either!

How's the tennis? Have you won any competitions this year? By the way, Jack's really good now. He might beat you this year!

Guess what? Lee asked Aneta to go out with him, and she said no! They had a big argument about it. They were both really upset but, luckily, they're friends again now. Maybe Aneta will change her mind one day – they get on really well and Lee is still in love with her.

Anyway, I must go and help mum with the dinner. Say hello to everyone.

Love,

Lauren

7D A Maori tradition

Reading

1 Work in pairs. Read the sentences. Are they true for your country?

1 People who break the law go to prison.
2 All criminals – teenagers or adults – are treated in the same way.
3 Criminals have meetings with the victim or the victim's family.

2 7.10 **Read the text and decide if the sentences in Exercise 1 are true for New Zealand.**

3 Read the text again and find out:

1 who the Maori people are.
2 what happens at a community meeting.
3 the results of community meetings.

4 Find words in the text that have similar meanings to the <u>underlined</u> words below.

1 We met <u>the people who live</u> in the town.
2 It's a <u>very old</u> system.
3 The police tried to find the <u>criminal</u>.
4 I need to <u>say sorry</u> to my friend.
5 That was the <u>most difficult</u> test I've ever done!

5 Work in groups of four. Do you think the Maori system is a good idea? Why? / Why not?

Culture

What usually happens to criminals? In the UK, when the police catch criminals, they go to court and then they usually go to prison. However, in New Zealand they have a different system for young people who break the law.

The system comes from the Maori people. They were the first inhabitants of New Zealand, and they have ancient and respected traditions. They understand that crime hurts many people: the victim, the victim's family, the criminal's family and the criminal too. In Maori society, when a young person breaks the law, the community has a meeting. The people who are affected by the crime sit down together and talk about the situation. In this way, young criminals understand the effects of their actions. They have to meet the person who they have hurt. For example, teenagers who have been in a fight have to face each other again and talk about the problem.

In the meetings, families decide what the young offender must do in order to compensate their victims. One of the most important things that the offender has to do is apologise to the victim. This is a very difficult and uncomfortable thing for most young offenders to do. If a teenager steals something from a classmate, the community asks him (or her) to say sorry to the classmate. Most young people say this is the hardest thing to do.

The Maori system helps young people to change their behaviour. It tries to bring something positive from a negative situation, and most of the time, it succeeds.

Listening

6 7.11 **Listen to an interview with Maori teenager, Meri Te Kanawa. Choose the correct answers (a, b or c).**

1 Maori teenagers …
- a enjoy hip-hop music.
- b are different to other teenagers.
- c don't like going out.

2 *Whanau* means …
- a family.
- b friends.
- c neighbours.

3 *Pakeha* means …
- a Maori gang.
- b European New Zealanders.
- c aunts and uncles.

4 The gangs in New Zealand are …
- a Pakeha.
- b Maori.
- c Pakeha and Maori.

Social science and English

Citizenship: helping others

1 **Work in pairs. How many charities or non-governmental organisations (NGOs) can you name? What do they do?**

2 **Read about the Prince's Trust and answer the questions.**

1 Who does the Prince's Trust help?
2 How does it help them?
3 Why is it called the Prince's Trust?

The Prince's Trust

Prince's Trust

About the Trust

The Prince's Trust is a youth charity that helps change young lives.

It gives practical and financial support, developing key workplace skills such as confidence and motivation. The trust works with 14 to 30-year-olds who have struggled at school, have no families, have not had a job for a long time, or have been in trouble with the law.

It has helped more than 575,000 young people since 1976 and supports 100 more each working day. More than three in four young people they helped last year moved into work, education or training.

Around one in five young people in the UK are not in work, education or training. Youth unemployment costs the UK economy £10 million a day in lost productivity, while youth crime costs £1 billion every year.

The Trust's history

The Prince's Trust was started in 1976 by the Prince of Wales. After he completed his duty in the Royal Navy, Prince Charles became dedicated to improving the lives of disadvantaged young people in the UK and began the Trust to carry out this work.

3 **Are there any charities similar to the Prince's Trust in your country? What do they do?**

Project

Work in groups. Write a questionnaire of 3–6 questions to find out what problems young people have in your community or at your school, and what changes people want. Write a paragraph about the results of your questionnaire.

TRUE STORY

A real pirate

1 What do you know about pirates? Discuss these questions with a partner before you read the article:

1 Who were pirates?
2 What was their lifestyle like?
3 What crimes do you think pirates committed?

2 Read all the information below and match the words (1–8) to their meanings (a–h).

1	setting off	a	having the ability
2	capable	b	the crime of disobeying the captain
3	missions	c	hard/unkind
4	raided	d	ways of dealing with criminals
5	punishments	e	attacked/robbed
6	cruel	f	kill
7	execute	g	beginning/leaving
8	mutiny	h	jobs/tasks

Sir Francis Drake

Born around 1541, Francis Drake soon learned to be an excellent sailor, **setting off** on his first voyage at the age of 12. He quickly became a **capable** and popular captain. His first **missions** were when his cousin asked him to join him sailing between England, Africa and the New World. Drake was one of the first British sailors to explore what is now North America, and the first to sail around the world. He also led England to victory in a war. Drake became rich and famous in England, where he is still considered a great hero.

But there is another side to this story. After Queen Elizabeth told him to become a privateer, Drake regularly **raided** ships and stole goods. In one raid, in 1580, he stole money worth €7,000,000 today. In another, he took 36 kilograms of gold, 13 chests full of treasure and 26 tons of silver! Drake was a pirate.

Unlike the romantic life that we see in films, a pirate's life was filled with dirt and disease, living in terrible conditions on ships with lots of rats. The **punishments** they used were very **cruel**. They were the thieves and murderers of the sixteenth century. We may never know what kind of a pirate Drake was. Most people said that he was not the worst, and there are many stories about his acts of kindness towards his victims. However, we do know that Drake ordered his men to **execute** Thomas Doughty, his friend and shipmate, for an act of **mutiny**. So it seems that even his friends were not safe around Drake!

Names given to pirates:
Privateers
Buccaneers
Corsairs
Swashbucklers
Freebooters
Filibusters

Some of the best-known and most feared pirates:
Blackbeard (Edward Teach)
Barbarossa (meaning Redbeard)
Henry Every
Henry Morgan
Bartholomew Roberts
Anne Bonny
Grace O'Malley
Jean Laffite

Timeline for Drake:
1541 – Drake is born in southern England
1573 – Drake's men steal 20 tons of gold and silver. Most of it is buried on the beach.
1581 – Drake becomes Sir Francis Drake.
1588 – Drake defends England.
1595 – Drake goes on his last voyage.
1596 – Drake dies and is buried at sea.

3 Now answer these questions.

1 What were Drake's main achievements?
2 In what ways was Drake a bad person?
3 In what ways was Drake not as bad as other pirates?

Travel

8

> Grammar

Learn about the second conditional, and quantifeirs *very, really, quite, a bit, a lot, much* + adjectives.

> Vocabulary

Learn words for holidays, holiday packing and transport.

Work with adjectives and adverbs, and verb + noun combinations.

> Skills

Read and do a quiz about survival, read about maps, and The Caribbean.

Listen to conversations about travel, and holidays.

Write an email with holiday tips.

> Communicate

Offering help, requesting information, giving advice, making suggestions, and giving instructions.

1 **Work in pairs. Imagine you are the people in the photo. Write your conversation.**

2 **Work in pairs. What are the best types of holiday for these people? Use ideas from the vocabulary box.**

families with young children	retired couples
groups of teenagers	school groups
people aged 18–30	young couples

adventure beach cruise day trip eco-tour family hotel package romantic safari sightseeing theme park trekking

3 8.1 **Listen to a customer at a travel agency. Which holidays does the travel agent suggest? Which holiday do you think is best for the customer?**

4 **What kinds of holiday have you been on? What kinds of holidays would you like to go on? Tell your partner.**

8A Survival

A

Speaking

1 Choose a holiday from the box on page 87. What are you going to take with you? Choose items from the below. Then compare your holiday and items with your partner's.

a compass a first aid kit a map a penknife
a phrasebook a rucksack a sleeping bag
a suitcase suncream a swimsuit a tent
a torch a water bottle waterproofs

2 Look at the other items in the box. Think of situations where they are useful. Compare with your partner.

Reading and listening

3 8.2 Read and listen to the text. Find three words which you don't understand. Work with other students to decide the meaning of the words.

4 Work in pairs and do the quiz. Compare your results.

NATIONAL GEOGRAPHIC
Explorer Journeys

Imagine going on your dream trip. Which of these comments sounds like you ?

A *'I like having fun. I would go to a beach and a theme park with my friends.'*
B *'I love danger and excitement. I would visit places nobody has ever been to.'*
C *'I like being comfortable. I would go on a cruise or to a luxury hotel.'*

Did you choose B? Perhaps you'd make a good National Geographic explorer. What do you think? Would you be cool in tough situations? Take our quiz and find out how well you'd survive a trip 'into the wild'.

Quiz questions

1 Look at picture A. Where would you be if this was the view from your tent?
  a I'd be in the Sahara desert.
  b I'd be on a beach in Scotland.

2 What would you do if you found a tarantula in your sleeping bag?
  a I'd calmly take a photo of it.
  b I'd scream loudly.

3 Look at picture B. Would you panic if you saw this in the water next to you?
  a Yes, I would! It's a box jellyfish, which is very dangerous!
  b No, I wouldn't. Jellyfish are harmless.

4 If you got lost at night up a mountain, what would you do?
  a I'd wait patiently for sunrise.
  b I'd try to get back to base quickly.

5 Look at picture C. If you were on an expedition to find the North Pole, which things would be the most useful?
  a A map of the stars, a water bottle and a penknife.
  b A compass, a mobile phone and a torch.

How did you do?

Mostly 'a's: You did well! You're knowledgeable and cool-headed. You'd make a good explorer.

Mostly 'b's: You like travelling dangerously! If the jellyfish didn't sting you, you'd probably have an accident running around mountains in the dark. Luckily, this is only a quiz!

B

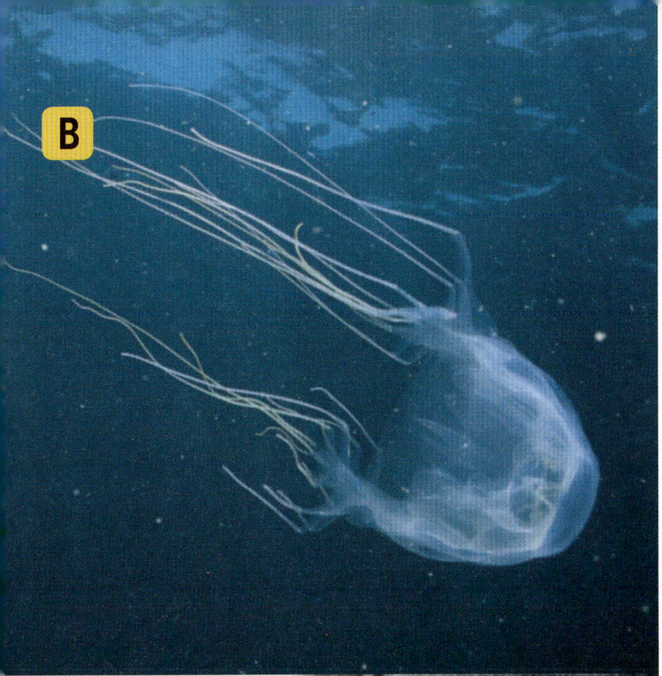

C

Working with words: adjective → adverb

5 **Look at the examples. Then find more adverbs in the text and answer key.**

loud	I'd scream loudly.
good	You did well.

See Working with words: Page 108

Grammar: second conditional

6 **Look at the introduction to the quiz and complete the table.**

Imaginary situation	Action
If I was on a dream holiday,	I .... to a beach. I .... visit places nobody has ever been to.

See Grammar Explorer: Page 126

7 **Look at the chart. Which tense do we use in the part of the sentence with *if* – the present simple or the past simple?**

8 **Read the quiz again. Then complete the table.**

Would you panic if you .... this in the water?	Yes, I .... No, I ....
What .... you .... if you found a tarantula?	I'd scream.

See Grammar Exlorer: Page 126

With pronouns, we often use the abbreviation *'d* for *would*: *I'd go, You'd go, He'd go, She'd go*, etc.

9 **Imagine you were on trip abroad. Complete the sentences using the second conditional.**

1 If I .... (**feel**) travel sick, I .... (**take**) a tablet.
2 I .... (**buy**) a phrase book if I .... (**not/speak**) the local language.
3 I .... (**not/panic**) if I .... (**get**) lost.
4 If I .... (**miss**) my train, I .... (**phone**) my parents.
5 If I .... (**lose**) my passport, I .... (**go**) to the police.

Speaking

10 **Write questions for the sentences in Exercise 9. Then think of two possible answers for each question.**

e.g. What would you do if you felt travel sick?

11 **Work in pairs. Ask and answer the questions from Exercise 10.**

A: *What would you do if you felt travel sick?*
B: *I'd go to sleep, or maybe I'd get some fresh air.*

12 **Read the advice from an experienced explorer. Complete the text with the correct form of the verbs.**

If I was on a trip to somewhere new, (**1**) .... (**I / not take**) any unnecessary risks. You should always plan carefully for the local conditions. For example, if (**2**) .... (**I / be**) in the Arctic, (**3**) .... (**I / wear**) special clothes because you can get frostbite very easily. If (**4**) .... (**we / go**) to an area we didn't know well, (**5**) .... (**we / ask**) local people about possible dangers. It's common sense. Even here in Europe, (**6**) .... (**I / not go**) walking without waterproofs, a basic first aid kit, and extra food. That way, if (**7**) .... (**I / have**) an accident, (**8**) .... (**I / be**) OK while I waited to be rescued.

Fast finishers

Find the nine letter word. How many words can you make with the letters?

E	D	R	V	A	N	U	T	E

8B Maps

How would we travel without maps? It would be a bit adventurous to set off from Oxford Circus to go to London Bridge if there wasn't a map of the London Underground at each station. In fact, a lot of the early map-makers were adventurers and explorers, especially in the 15th and 16th centuries.

So what did people do before there were maps? Well, it was quite easy to use natural features like mountains and valleys if you were travelling on foot or riding a horse. People sailed small boats down rivers and followed coastlines. And it was much more logical to use time, not distance, to measure journeys: the next village is a three-hour ride, for example. In some cultures, people used spoken instructions to pass on information, like the 'song lines' of the Aboriginal Australians, and special poetry in India.

In fact, in the earliest maps, people didn't draw landmarks. They drew the arrangement of the stars. It was very easy to see the night sky and use it for navigation. The sky was a lot clearer before the light pollution from cities that we have today. When towns and cities were built, people drew road maps which gave correct distances and directions.

The London Underground was opened in 1863 and it also used a road map style. But a man called Henry Beck realised that travelling by train isn't the same as driving your car across London. Passengers only needed to know which stations to change at. His new design for the Underground map wasn't very popular with the train companies at first. But the passengers loved it and in 1933, 700,000 copies were printed.

These days, of course, you can ride a bike, fly a micro-light or trek across a desert and know your exact position, using a GPS. It's really difficult to get lost!

Working with words: verb + noun

1 Look at the examples. Think of two more nouns we often use after *ride* and *drive*.

I ride a bike to school.

My dad drives a lorry at work.

See Working with words: Page 108

Speaking

2 Look at the words in the box. How many other forms of transport do you know?

a canoe a catamaran a ferry a hovercraft
a jeep a lorry a mountain bike a ship
a taxi a tram the underground

3 Work in pairs. How many different forms of transport you would have to use to get from your town to London? Use some of the verbs in the box below and the nouns in Exercise 2. Repeat for three more destinations around the world.

e.g. A: *First, we would take a bus to the airport.*

B: *OK, but first I would ride my bike to the bus station.*

climb cycle drive fly hike
ride sail take trek walk

Listening

4 8.3 Listen to three conversations (1–3). Where are the people? There is one extra place.

an airport a ferry a taxi
an underground railway station

5 8.3 Listen again and complete the information.

1 Train line: the .... Ticket price: ....
2 Flight time: .... Gate number: ....
3 Arrival time: .... Price of ticket: ....

6 Match these notices to two of the places in Exercise 4.

1 Don't throw littler into the water.

2 *Please do not talk to the driver during the journey.*

Reading and listening

7 STUDY SKILLS **Read the text quickly and choose the best title.**

a The London Underground
b How to travel without a map
c A history of maps

8 8.4 STUDY SKILLS **Read and listen to the text. Complete the sentences.**

1 It wasn't .... to use natural features for navigation.
2 These days, we .... see as many stars in the sky because of light pollution.
3 The train companies didn't .... Beck's new map at first.

Grammar: quantifiers and adjectives

9 Read the text again and complete these sentences.

1 It would be .... adventurous to set off from Oxford Circus.
2 In fact, ... the early map-makers were adventurers and explorers.
3 It was .... easy to use natural features.
4 It was .... more logical to use time.
5 His new design wasn't .... popular at first.
6 It's .... difficult to get lost!

See Grammar Explorer: Page 126

10 Complete the chart below with *a lot, much, really, quite* and *very*.

.... a bit	+ adjective
.... a bit	+ comparative adjective

11 Choose the correct option.

1 Trekking in the Himalayas would be **very / a lot** dangerous.
2 A beach holiday would be **quite / much** boring.
3 A cruise around the Mediterranean would be **a lot / really** interesting.
4 A safari would be **much / very** better than a trip to a theme park.
5 A train journey would be **a bit / very** more exciting than a helicopter trip.

Speaking

12 Work in groups of four. Discuss the sentences in Exercise 11. Do you agree with the opinions? Why? / Why not?

Study skills

Reading a text

1 Before you read a text, you should know why you are reading it. Which of these things do you want to do?

- answer a question
- look for detailed information
- get the general idea/topic
- find out the writer's purpose
- learn new vocabulary
- read for pleasure

2 Choose a helpful strategy for your purpose. Look through the study skills boxes in previous units to help you.

8C At the hotel

Reading and listening

1 8.5 **Read and listen to the dialogue. What is the problem?**

- **a** Jack can't find Lee.
- **b** Aneta has lost the room key.
- **c** They don't know where their teachers is.

2 Read the dialogue again. Where have Jack, Aneta and Lauren looked for Mrs Taylor? Why are they looking for her?

3 In the dialogue, which expressions are used for …

offering help?
requesting information?
giving advice?
making suggestions?
giving instructions?

4 8.6 **Listen and repeat the *Useful expressions*. Focus on your intonation.**

USEFUL EXPRESSIONS

Could you give us the room number of Mrs Taylor, please?
Don't turn left or you'll be in the kitchens!
If I were you, I'd look in the restaurant.
Make sure he's OK.
What can I do for you?
Why don't you leave a message?
Would you like me to call the room?
You should go back to your room.

Receptionist:	Hello. What can I do for you?
Jack:	Could you give us the room number of Mrs Taylor, please?
Receptionist:	Is she a guest here at the hotel?
Lauren:	Yes, she's our teacher.
Receptionist:	And the arrival date?
Jack:	We arrived yesterday.
Receptionist:	Here we are … room 602. Would you like me to call the room?
Aneta:	Yes, please. That would be great.
Receptionist:	There's no answer. She's not in her room, I'm sorry.
Lauren:	Oh dear. We need to speak to her.
Receptionist:	If I were you, I'd look in the restaurant. She's probably having breakfast.
Aneta:	We've been there already. She's not there.
Lauren:	And she's not in the gift shop either.
Receptionist:	Why don't you leave a message for her? I wouldn't worry if I were you.
Jack:	It's all right, thanks. We'll manage.
Receptionist:	Oh, have you tried the gym?
Aneta:	No … can you tell us where it is?
Receptionist:	Go through those doors and down the stairs. Don't turn left or you'll be in the kitchens!
Lauren:	Thanks. Jack, you should go back to your room and look after Lee. Make sure he's OK. We'll look in the gym.

5 **Match the questions (1–5) with the answers (a–f). There is one extra answer.**

1 Could you tell me where the gift shop is, please?
2 Would you like me to help carry your bags?
3 What's the best way of getting to the zoo?
4 Oh, it's raining. Perhaps a river trip isn't a good idea.
5 How do I make a call from my room?

a Dial zero, and then dial the number you want to call.
b If I were you, I'd take the underground.
c You should set off as soon as possible.
d Yes, certainly. It's next to the restaurant.
e Yes, please. They're quite heavy.
f Why don't you go to the Natural History Museum instead?

6 8.7 **Listen to a conversation (1) and an answerphone message (2), and complete the information.**

	1	2
Guest's name:	....	Mrs Watson
Type of room:	single	?
Length of stay:	....	....
Arrival date:	....	....

Speaking

7 **Work in pairs. You are the receptionist and a guest at a hotel in London. Write dialogues for the situations in the box. Then take a role each and practise your dialogues.**

You've lost your passport.
There's a spider in your bath.
You need advice about sightseeing.
You want to change some money.

Pronunciation: difficult words

8 **How do you pronounce these words? Compare with your partner.**

beautiful biscuit business calm castle comfortable foreign mountain woman women

9 8.8 **Listen and repeat the words in Exercise 8.**

Writing: holiday tips

1 **Read Ben's tips for Lee's trip to the USA. Which of these things does he talk about?**

money packing passports sightseeing tickets vaccinations

2 **Find these words in the email. Which tenses follow them?**

unless in case or

See Grammar Explorer: Page 127

3 **Complete the sentences with *unless, in case* and *or.***

1 You'll need a return ticket .... you won't be allowed into the country.
2 You won't be allowed in .... you have a return ticket.
3 Take some travel tablets .... you get travel sick.

4 **Write tips for travellers to your country or to a country you know. Use the ideas in Exercise 1 to help you.**

Hi Lee,

I'm really pleased that you're coming to the States this summer. It'll be great! There's lots to do, so you should start to get organised. The first thing is to check that your passport is valid or you won't be able to get into the country. That would be terrible! I don't think you'll need a visa unless you stay for more than three months. (It would be great if you could, but I guess two weeks is good too.) What else? It's a good idea to change some money before you come. And bring some hiking gear in case we decide to go camping. And don't forget your camera or you won't have any sightseeing photos to show your mum when you get back! Anyway, I'll write more later. Here's my cellphone number (7955846745) in case you want to text me.

See you soon,
Ben

8D The Caribbean

Reading

1 **Work in pairs. Look at the photos. Would you like to go to these places and do these things? Why? / Why not?**

Culture

The Caribbean is many people's idea of paradise – beautiful beaches, fantastic wildlife and great weather. But what's it like to live there?

The original name of Jamaica meant 'land of wood and water', but perhaps it should be 'land of music and sport'. Bob Marley was probably the most famous reggae musician in the world, and Jamaica is also the home of athletes Usain Bolt and Asafa Powell. But unfortunately not everybody can be world-famous. Most people work in jobs that are related to the tourist industry or farming. So although Jamaica is a beautiful place, people who want to do something different with their lives often emigrate to the USA or the UK.

It's a good idea to learn to swim if you live in the Bahamas. But you shouldn't be afraid of sharks. The sea around the islands is crystal clear and quite shallow, which is perfect for sharks. The Bahamas is one of the few places in the world where you can swim with (and feed!) sharks. The fishing and diving resorts attract a lot of tourists, and the islands' economy depends on this kind of tourism. Local businesses have to work hard to protect this natural environment.

A new kind of tourism called 'eco-tourism' is increasing in some parts of the Caribbean. It focuses on giving employment to local young people so that they don't need to emigrate. In the Virgin Islands, for example, the Sustainable Farm Institute on St. Croix is an alternative to more traditional tourist resorts. Local people learn how to start their own farms – which will give their families work in the future – and tourists come to stay on the farm and experience more than just a beach holiday.

2 (CD 8.9) **Read about some of the Caribbean islands. Where would you go to do these things?**

1 feed a shark
2 have an 'eco-holiday'
3 stay on a working farm
4 see the homes of famous musicians

3 **Read the text again and answer the questions.**

1 Why do people from Jamaica go to the USA or the UK?
2 What kinds of activities do tourists go to the Bahamas for?
3 Find two reasons why eco-tourism is good for the Virgin Islands.

4 **Find words in the text which match the definitions.**

1 leave your country to live in a different one
2 not very deep
3 the money of a country
4 jobs and work

Listening

5 (CD 8.10) **Listen to Paul talking about his holiday in the Caribbean and answer the questions.**

1 Where did Paul stay?
 a At a friend's house.
 b In a hotel.
 c On a farm.
2 What was different about his holiday?
 a He worked.
 b It was free.
 c He never went to the beach.
3 Where did he go at the end of his holiday?
 a On a fishing trip.
 b To a tropical forest.
 c To the capital city.

Geography and English

Geotourism

1 **What do you think 'geotourism' is? Choose the correct option (a, b or c).**

a Visits to volcanoes and other geological sites of interest.
b Tourism which protects natural places such as forests.
c Tourism which doesn't harm places where tourists go.

2 **Read about Geotourism and check your answer to Exercise 1.**

What is the Geotourism Challenge?

The National Geographic Society organises a competition every year. It looks at tourist resorts around the world and chooses the ones which are most successful in *geotourism*. Recently the Sustainable Farm Institute in the Virgin Islands was a finalist in the competition.

» *What is Geotourism?*

Geotourism is a kind of tourism that protects and respects the places where tourists go. *Ecotourism* focuses on the natural environment. *Geotourism* also protects historic sites and local culture. It is a kind of tourist activity that helps local people and their economy but does not destroy it.

» *What are Geotourism projects?*

These are places where geotourism is already successful – where local governments, tourist businesses and local people work together to develop their tourist industry. There are also 'planned projects', where people have agreed to the ideas, but they are still developing their geotourism activities.

3 **Look at the map and the key. What happens at the places marked by the coloured dots?**

Project

Work in groups. Make a list of the main tourist areas in your area or country. Then find or draw a map and mark the different kinds of tourism on the map.

Consolidation Units 7 and 8

Reading

Identifying the writer's purpose

- Read the task and find the language functions.
- Think of expressions that are used with these functions.

1 Read Dan's email to Jenny. Why has he written to her? Which expression gives you the answer?

a to apologise for something
b to ask for help
c to give her advice

Hi Jenny,

Do you remember the Saturday job I told you about? I'm going to apply for it. The application form is complicated. Could you help me with it? You're good at this kind of thing. Can I come your house at the weekend?

Dan

2 What expressions can you think of for these functions?

1 asking for advice
2 making a suggestion
3 agreeing with somebody

3 Match the notes (1–2) with the writers' purpose (a–c). There is one extra purpose.

1

Hi Dan
No problem, I'm happy to help. Why don't you come round on Saturday morning?
See you then.
Jenny

2

Hi Jenny,
I'm glad you enjoyed the film last night. Me too. And you're right, it's a great idea to go and see it again!
Lisa

a to make a suggestion
b to ask for advice
c to agree with somebody

Listening

Identifying the situation

- Read the task instruction and the options.
- Try to predict words and expressions you might hear in each situation.
- Listen for key words and expressions.

Important! If you can listen for a second time, don't forget to check your answers.

1 Think of words and expressions you might hear in conversations in these places.

1 at a hotel reception desk
2 at a theatre booking office
3 at a railway station
4 in a restaurant

2 Where would you hear people say these things?

a I'd like the soup, please.
b I'm sorry, there aren't any tickets left.
c How many nights are you staying?
d Do you want a single or a return ticket?

3 Think of questions for *a* and *b*, and responses for *c* and *d* in Exercise 2.

4 8.11 **Listen to the conversations and match them with three of the places in Exercise 1.**

5 8.12 **Listen to the announcement. Which group of words do you hear?**

a flight passengers gate
b passenger train late
c Manchester delay buses

6 Where is the announcement in Exercise 5?

a at an airport
b at a railway station
c at a bus station

7 8.13 **Listen to the answerphone message. Where is it from? Choose the correct option (a–c).**

a a hotel
b a travel agency
c a clothes shop

Possessive adjectives and possessive pronouns

This is her bike. = This bike is hers.

1 Read the first sentence. Complete the second sentence with a possessive pronoun.

1 The blue bike is Ben's. It's ....
2 This is our dog. She's ....
3 'Is this your book?' 'Yes, it's ....'
4 'Is that their house?' 'Yes, it's ....'
5 Is this your jacket? Or is the green one............. ?
6 The red hat is Emma's. It's ....

There + *be* and *It* + *be*

We use *there* to introduce something. We use *it* when we refer to the thing for a second time. We also use *it* + *be* with adjectives and prepositions.

2 Choose the correct words.

(**1**) **There / It** was very hot yesterday. (**2**) **There / It** was a fire in the forest. (**3**) **There / It** was very dangerous. (**4**) **There / It** was very difficult to put out the fire. (**5**) **There / It** was a special report about it on TV.

3 Complete the dialogue with *there* or *it*.

Joe: Hey, (**1**) ....'s a writing competition at school.
Emma: I know! (**2**) ....'s on the school website.
Joe: Is (**3**) .... a good prize?
Emma: Yes, (**4**) ....'s a trip to an outdoor centre called *Wild Skills*.
Joe: Oh, yes. (**5**) ....'s a great climbing wall there. I read about it.
Emma: So, let's have a go!

Like, be like, look like, to like

We use *like* in different ways.
My brother (a) looks like me, but he (b) isn't like me. He (c) likes playing tennis and I like playing team games, (d) like football.

4 Complete the table with *a*, *b*, *c* and *d* to match the examples of *like* in the sentences above.

....	to like = a verb
....	like = for example
....	to look like = physical appearance
....	be like = to be similar

5 Complete the sentences.

1 .... you .... science fiction?
2 Who .... you .... in your family?
3 .... your sister .... you? Or are you very different?
4 Is that Matt Damon? It .... him.
5 Food .... chips and chocolate is fattening.

6 Match the questions (1–4) with the answers (a–d).

1 What does a tarantula look like?
2 What are tarantulas like?
3 Do you like tarantulas?
4 Would you like a tarantula?

a It's hairy, and it has eight legs.
b No, thanks.
c They're quite frightening, but they aren't always dangerous.
d Yes, I think they're interesting.

7 Write questions for these answers. Use a *snake* or *snakes* in each question.

1 .... ?
No, I don't think they would be good pets.
2 .... ?
They are long and thin.
3 .... ?
No, I don't. I think they're frightening.
4 .... ?
I think some of them can be aggressive.

Review Units 7 and 8

Vocabulary

1 Write the words.

1 An area with lots of shops. s............. c.............
2 Stealing from shops. s.............
3 Rubbish that people drop in the street. l.............
4 People who break the law. c.............
5 A place for professional football, etc. s............. s.............

1 mark per item: .../5 marks

2 Write the types of holiday.

1 On a ...., you see wild animals.
2 On a ...., you live on a ship.
3 There's sea and sand on a .... holiday.
4 On a .... holiday, you visit places of interest.
5 On .... holidays, you walk a lot.

1 mark per item: .../5 marks

3 Write the things.

1 ....
2 ....
3 ....
4 ....
5 ....

1 mark per item: .../5 marks

4 Write the transport.

1 ....
2 ....
3 ....
4 ....
5 ....

1 mark per item: .../5 marks

5 Complete the sentences.

1 I broke my watch, so I .... this one from my friend.
2 Somebody .... the bank. They took all the money.
3 .... the news on TV at 6 p.m.?
4 'Does she speak French .... ?' 'Yes, she's fluent.'
5 I learned to .... a bike when I was six.

1 mark per item: .../5 marks

Grammar

6 Report a teacher's words with the verbs.

1 'Sit down, everyone.' (**order**)
2 'Don't make a noise.' (**tell / the class**)
3 'Please listen, Jack.' (**ask**)
4 'Don't cheat in the test!' (**warn / the class**)
5 'Would you like to come to a meeting?' (**invite / the parents**)

1 mark per item: .../5 marks

7 Are the questions correct (✓) or incorrect (✗)?

1 Can you tell us where is the conference?
2 Do you know is there a skate park near here?
3 Could you tell me how much the train tickets are?
4 Can you tell me if pets are allowed here?
5 Do you know what time the shops close?

1 mark per item: .../5 marks

8 Write statements or questions using the second conditional.

1 If I .... a tarantula, I'd run away. (**see**)
2 I .... to Africa if I had enough money. (**go**)
3 If I was an explorer, I .... in this country. (**not / live**)
4 If I .... to Egypt, I'd visit the pyramids. (**go**)
5 What .... if you were lost in the Arctic? (**do**)

1 mark per item: .../5 marks

9 Choose the correct options.

1 It's **a bit / much** boring to watch TV all day.
2 A cruise is **quite / much** more expensive than a camping holiday.
3 Climbing Mount Etna would be **a lot / quite** dangerous.
4 Horses are **much / very** faster than mountain bikes.
5 A trip around the world would be **a lot / really** exciting.

1 mark per item: .../5 marks

10 Complete the sentences.

1 This camera is John's. It's ....
2 This is our house. It's ....
3 .... was a hurricane in the Caribbean yesterday.
4 That woman .... like Madonna! They're really similar!
5 Ben .... like his brother. They're both competitive.

1 mark per item: .../5 marks

Communicate

11 Complete the dialogue with the expressions.

Could you give him a message?
You're welcome.
I'll tell him.
Can you ask him to…
With pleasure.

John:	Is Ben there, please?
Ben's mum:	No, he's not here at the moment.
John:	(**1**) ....
Ben's mum:	(**2**) ....
John:	(**3**) .... call John, please?
Ben's mum:	Yes, of course. Has he got your phone number?
John:	Yes, he has. But if it's really late, he can send me a text.
Ben's mum:	OK, (**4**) ....
John:	Thanks very much.
Ben's mum:	(**5**) ....

2 marks per item: …/10 marks

12 Match the expressions with the functions.

1 Why don't you go by bus?
2 Could you tell me the flight number?
3 If I were you, I'd take a train.
4 Go to Gate 45, in the North terminal.
5 Can I help you with your suitcase?

a giving advice
b making a suggestion
c offering help
d requesting information
e giving instructions

2 marks per item: …/10 marks

13 Are the underlined sounds in each pair the same (S) or different (D)?

1	woman	women	....
2	mountain	listen	....
3	comfortable	table	....
4	business	bus	....
5	calm	arm	....

2 marks per item: …/10 marks

14 Complete the sentences with *or*, *in case* or *unless*.

1 I'm packing some waterproofs .... it rains.
2 Hurry up .... we'll miss the bus.
3 We won't phone you .... we have a problem.
4 Take some insect repellent .... there are mosquitoes.
5 You can't get on the plane .... you have a ticket.

2 marks per item: …/10 marks

15 Complete the email with the words in the box.

a lot **actually** **at** **by the way**
if I were you **guess what** **luckily**
really **to** **unfortunately**

Dear Lisa,

I'm (**1**) .... pleased that you're coming to visit us! (**2**) .... , I'd take the bus. It's (**3**) .... cheaper than the train. (**4**) .... , it's quicker too. (**5**) .... , there's only one bus a day. I'll come and meet you (**6**) .... the bus station. (**7**) .... ! I've just dyed my hair. I'm blonde now! You might not recognise me!

(**8**) .... , I hope you like cats – we've got four now. They sometimes fight, but (**9**) .... they spend a lot of time outside! Don't forget (**10**) .... send me the dates of your visit!

Love,
Billie

1 mark per item: …/10 marks

Total: …/100

I can...

I can give and take messages.
I can offer help.
I can request information.
I can give advice.
I can make suggestions.
I can give instructions.

A questionnaire

What would you do if ... ?

Name: *Sylvia O'Donnell*
Age: *17*

TRAVEL

If you could be anywhere in the world right now, where would you be?
That's easy. I'd be at home with my family.
Wouldn't you choose to be on an island paradise?
No! I would like to visit the Caribbean one day maybe, but right now, if I could, I would go home!
So, where else in the world would you like to go?
If I could, I would visit China or Japan.
Would you ever consider being a space tourist – flying to the moon, for example?
No way! I'd be too scared.

TRANSPORT

How would you like to get around?
I would like to have enough money to take a taxi when I need one.
What kind of car would you like to have?
I'd have a Ferrari ... and motorbikes ... I'd like to have some old motorbikes!
Where would you keep them all?
I'd need a big garage, wouldn't I?

HOUSE

Where would you like to live and what would the house be like?
I'd live by the sea if I could. I'd have a big house with huge balconies so I could sit and look at the waves. Sounds nice! If I could, I'd have a house in the mountains too, with a fireplace in every room! And a flat in New York!

MONEY

If you became very rich tomorrow, what would you do first?
I'd buy a house first – then a car. Then I'd give some money to my parents and my sisters.
Would you give any money to friends or strangers?
I think so. If I was very rich, I would like to help people. I would pay for a children's hospital.

AMBITION

What would you like to do with your life?
If I could, I would like to become a doctor.
Would you like to get married and have children?
Not for a long time. I want to enjoy myself and start my career first.

1 Read the questionnaire and Sylvia's answers. Then find...

a all the questions using *would*.
b examples of the second conditional in Sylvia's answers.

e.g. ... If I could, I would go home!

2 Make more questions using these words. How would *you* answer these questions?

1 How / you like / change your appearance?
2 What / you like / study?
3 When / you like / get married?
4 If you / need / advice, who / you call?
5 If you / have / €1,000, what / you buy?
6 If you / leave / your school, how / you feel?

Project

Write your own questionnaire.

- Choose *who* you want to ask
- Write your questions for that person (remember to use the second conditional)
- Ask your questions (you can do this by telephone or email if the person lives far away)
- Write down their answers
- Write the questions and answers together
- Add a photograph of the person

1 Working with words

positive adjective → negative adjective

We add *un-* or *im-* to some adjectives to give the opposite meaning.

friendly

unfriendly

1 Look at the table and then choose the correct option below.

un-	im-
uncomfortable unfriendly unhappy unhealthy unimportant unkind unlucky unnecessary untidy	immature impatient impolite impossible

1. I'm **lucky / unlucky**. I always win.
2. Wait a moment! Don't be **patient / impatient**.
3. Are you OK? You don't seem **happy / unhappy**.
4. It's **polite / impolite** to say 'thank you'.
5. Mrs Jones is very **kind / unkind** and helpful.

2 Complete the sentences with adjectives from the table in Exercise 1.

1. This sofa is very ....
2. I can't do this maths homework. It's .... !
3. I love chocolate and other .... food.
4. My brother is 16, but he's very ....
5. You don't have to do this. It's ....
6. Your bedroom is a mess. It's ....
7. Your neighbours never speak to you. They're ....
8. It doesn't matter. It's ....

Working on your own

3 What are the negative forms of these adjectives? We add *in-* or *ir-* to some of them. Check in a dictionary.

available correct intelligent
natural regular romantic

do and *make*

We use *do* and *make* with different nouns.

We're doing a project.

I'm making a cake.

1 Look at the table and then choose the correct option below.

do	make
an exam an experiment exercise history homework gymnastics maths a project sports a test the shopping the washing up	a cake a mess a mistake a model a noise a phone call a pizza a sandwich a sculpture breakfast friends my bed

1. We often use **do / make** with schoolwork.
2. We often use **do / make** with food and meals.

2 Complete the sentences with *do* or *make*.

1. Do you .... gymnastics at school?
2. Can you .... a pizza?
3. Do you have to .... an exam today?
4. When do you .... your homework?
5. What subjects do you .... at school?

3 Write sentences about your family.

e.g. My dad does the washing up.

1. .... my bed.
2. .... breakfast.
3. .... cakes.
4. .... the shopping.

Working on your own

4 Write your own sentence with *do* or *make* and each of these words.

exercises a mistake a phone call a project

2 Working with words

nouns → adjectives

We can add endings to nouns to make adjectives.
artist – artistic
fame – famous
success – successful
talent – talented
tradition – traditional

1 Make adjectives from these nouns and then complete the table.

danger interest music symbol use

artistic .... volcanic	.... famous poisonous	.... surprised talented
beautiful industrial successful	logical .... traditional tropical	

Note the spelling changes: beauty – beautiful, fame – famous.

2 Which adjectives from the table in Exercise 1 can you use to describe these people and things?

1 pop singers
2 classical music
3 mobile phones
4 film stars
5 Formula 1

3 Complete the sentences with adjectives from the table in Exercise 1.

1 My ambition is to be a .... musician.
2 I was .... when I won the talent competition.
3 A bite from a .... snake can kill you.
4 Hurricanes are a kind of .... storm.
5 Hamburgers are .... of the USA.

Working on your own

4 Make adjectives from these nouns. Check in a dictionary.

adventure energy environment power virus

5 Choose five adjectives from the table in Exercise 1. Write your own sentence with each adjective.

nouns and verbs → nouns

We can add endings to nouns and verbs to make nouns.
guitar – guitarist, sing – singing

1 Complete the words in the table.

Nouns		Nouns
art a cycle science	-ist	an art............. a cyclist a scientist
drums a trumpet	-er	a drummer a trumpet.............
Verbs		**Nouns**
communicate compete connect educate exhibit protect construct pollute	-ion	communication a competition a connect............. educat............. an exhibit............. protect............. construct............. pollution
paint write	-ing	painting writing
compose conduct paint perform play ski write	-er / -or	a composer a conductor a paint............. a perform............. a play............. a skier a write.............
perform appear	-ance	a performance an appearance

2 Choose the correct answers.

1 A pop concert is **a competition / an exhibition / a performance**.
2 Building a house is **protection / construction / pollution**.
3 Pictures in a gallery are **a competition / an exhibition / an appearance**.
4 A musician, singer, actor or dancer is a **conductor / performer / player**.
5 A telephone conversation is **an appearance / a communication / an education**.

Working on your own

3 Write new nouns from these words. Use a dictionary.

a harp a piano dance infect vaccinate

3 Working with words

noun + noun

We can use two nouns together to make another noun. This is called a compound noun.

skin + cream = skin cream

lunch + time = lunchtime

1 Match these nouns to make compound nouns. Which compound noun is one word?

art	bed	food	music	rugby
gallery	room	room	team	technology

2 Complete the compound nouns in the table with these words.

food infection killer player story virus

Two words	One word
cough medicine	earache
energy drink	earphones
flu	headache
junk	holidaymaker
news	pain ....
skin cream	toothache
skin	
tennis	

3 Look at the table in Exercise 2 and find the names of these things.

Working on your own

4 Choose five nouns from the tables in Exercises 1 and 2. Write your own sentence with each noun.

adjective + preposition

We often use prepositions after adjectives of emotions and feelings.

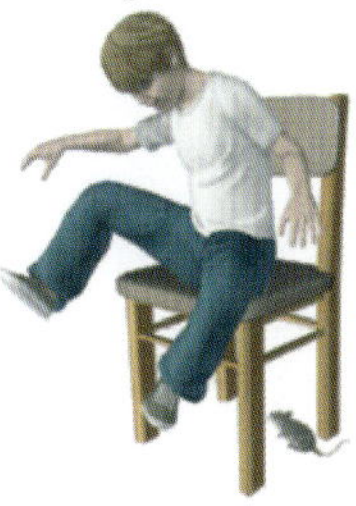

He's afraid of mice.

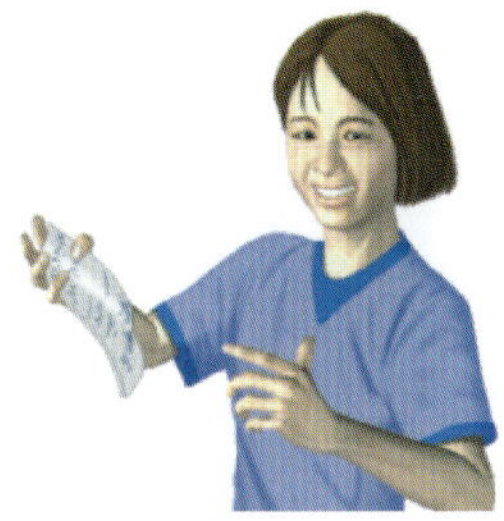

She's pleased with her grade.

1 Complete the second sentence with an appropriate expression from the table.

afraid of	frightened of
angry with	good at
annoyed with	happy about / with
bad at	interested in
bored with	pleased with
confused by	tired of
fed up with	worried about

1 My dad likes science.
He's ....

2 I didn't understand the beginning of the film.
I was ....

3 I always get bad grades in maths.
I'm ....

4 I think my friend needs some help.
I'm ....

5 I usually win in tennis matches.
I'm ....

2 Some expressions have similar meanings. Which expressions can you also use in these sentences?

1 Are you frightened of vaccinations?
2 Are you happy with your grades?
3 Are you tired of this exercise?
4 Are you angry with anyone at the moment?

Working on your own

3 Do you know what these adjective + preposition combinations mean? Check in a dictionary and write your own sentences with each combination.

ashamed of excited about nervous about proud of scared of

4 Working with words

adjective + noun

There are some adjectives and nouns that we often use together.

a digital camera

a wild animal

1 Answer the questions below with words and phrases from the table.

a bad habit	a living thing
a bad mood	a natural disaster
a best friend	a mobile phone
a digital camera	a tropical disease
free time	a violent movement
global warming	volcanic activity
a healthy lifestyle	a volcanic eruption
human activity	a wild animal
the industrial age	

1 What are lions, tigers and giraffes?
2 What are volcanoes, floods and hurricanes?
3 When did people start producing greenhouse gases?
4 How were the Canary Islands formed?

2 Complete the questions with words from the table in Exercise 1.

1 Have you got a .... lifestyle?
2 Do you tell your .... friend everything?
3 Do you have a lot of .... time at the weekend?
4 What are your .... habits?
5 Have you got a .... phone?

3 Cover the table in Exercise 1. Complete the adjective + noun combinations. Then check your answers.

1 a digital
2 global
3 a living
4 a tropical

Working on your own

4 Write your own sentence with each combination in Exercise 3.

false friends

False friends are words that look similar to words in your language, but they don't mean the same thing.

1 Choose the correct meanings.

1 an apartment:
 a a room
 b a home, on one floor with lots of rooms
2 a criminal:
 a a person who breaks the law
 b a detective story
3 a gymnasium:
 a a school
 b a place to do gymnastics
4 a habit:
 a a regular activity **b** type of clothes
5 polo:
 a a kind of T-shirt **b** a sport
6 smoking:
 a what you do with cigarettes
 b men's clothes

2 Match the words (1–4) with the pictures (a–d).

1 an athlete
2 an audience
3 chips
4 a record

3 Do you know what these words mean? Check in a dictionary.

argument audition data direction evidence extra novel objective obligation scenery

Working on your own

4 Make a note of any new false friends. Find new ways to remember the different meanings.

5 Working with words

compound adjectives

Compound adjectives are made of two words. The words are connected by a hyphen (-).

He seems bad-tempered.

He's always well-dressed.

1 Complete the adjectives in the table with these words.

dressed eyed looking minded

bad-tempered	old-fashioned
blue	open ....
brown-haired	self-centred
easy-going	self-confident
good	solar-powered
high-heeled	three-storey
new-age	well ....
	world-famous

2 Complete the sentences with adjectives from the table in Exercise 1.

1. Your dad accepts new ideas.
   He's ....
2. Your mum prefers things / ideas from the past.
   She's ....
3. Your sister thinks about herself a lot.
   She's ....
4. Your parents let you do what you want.
   They're ....
5. Your brother isn't afraid of new situations.
   He's ....

3 Work in pairs. Name a person or thing for each adjective. You must agree.

good-looking new-age solar-powered three-storey world-famous

Working on your own

4 Choose five adjectives from the table in Exercise 1 and write your own sentences.

phrasal verbs for relationships

Phrasal verbs have two parts: a verb and a preposition. The meaning is usually different from the meaning of the two parts on their own.

I broke my leg.

I broke up with my boyfriend.

1 Match the phrasal verbs (1–8) with the meanings (a–h).

1 break up	**a** argue with somebody
2 fall out	**b** have a romantic relationship
3 get on	**c** end a relationship
4 go out	**d** have a good relationship
5 make up	**e** make friends again after an argument
6 look after	**f** respect somebody
7 look up to	**g** have a similar appearance or personality as a relative
8 take after	**h** watch or protect

2 Complete the paragraph with phrasal verbs.

Rose and Thomas met at school. They (**1**) .... well. After a few weeks, they started to (**2**) .... with each other. But they often (**3**) .... and eventually they (**4**) .... I don't think they will (**5**) ....

3 Complete the sentences with the prepositions.

1. I look .... my big brother - he's great.
2. My mum looked .... me when I was ill.
3. I take .... my dad – were both tall.

Working on your own

4 Match these verbs and prepositions. Use two prepositions twice. Then check your answers in a dictionary.

break	after
fall	on
get	out
go	up
make	
take	

6 Working with words

verb + preposition

Some verbs are followed by prepositions.

I'm thinking about my lunch.

I'm talking to my best friend.

1 Complete the table with *of*, *with* and *to*.

agree	learn about
apologise for	pay for
argue with	talk about
believe in	talk ....
come from	think about
complain about	think of
consist	wait for
fight with	work on
know about	worry about

2 Complete the sentences with prepositions.

1. I don't fight .... my brother.
2. Do you believe .... ghosts?
3. My sister never agrees .... me.
4. Who do you argue .... most?

3 Choose the correct preposition.

1. 'What do you think **about / of** the Star Trek film?'
   'It's good.'
2. 'What are you thinking **about / of**?'
   'My lunch.'
3. 'Who are you talking **about / to**?'
   'My sister. She's phoning from London.'
4. 'What are you talking **about / to**?'
   'The Star Trek film.'

4 Complete the sentences with different verbs. The preposition is the same in each case.

1. I don't .... anything about Mars.
2. We .... about volcanoes today.
3. Don't .... about me. I'm fine.

Working on your own

5 Write your own sentences with each verb + preposition combination.

come from   complain about   work on

phrasal verbs

Phrasal verbs have two parts: a verb and a preposition. The meaning is usually different from the meaning of the two parts on their own.

Switch the TV on.
Switch the TV off.

Turn the sound up.
Turn the sound down.

1 Complete the requests below with phrasal verbs from the table.

come back	pick up	take over
find out	set off	turn up
get back	switch off	turn down
go back	switch on	

1. That's very loud! Could you .... the volume, please?
2. It's dark. .... a light.
3. Class is finished. .... your computers now.
4. I can't hear the TV. Can you .... the sound?

2 Read the first sentence. Choose the correct option.

1. Robots are taking over the world.
   They are in **control / exploring**.
2. How did you find out his telephone number?
   How did you **phone / discover** it?
3. What time did you set off this morning?
   When did you **drive / leave**?
4. I'll pick up my DVD from your house tonight.
   I'll **choose / collect** them.

3 Match the sentences (1–3) with the responses (a–c).

1. My parents have gone on holiday.
2. My cousins from Canada are visiting us.
3. I leave for school at 8.30.

a. What time do you get back?
b. When are they coming back?
c. When are they going back?

Working on your own

4 Write your own sentences to show the meaning of each phrasal verb.

set off   come back   pick up

7 Working with words

words that are easy to confuse

There are some words which mean different things but are easy to confuse.

The sun rises in the east.

Raise your arms.

1 Match the sentences (1–5) with the pictures (a–e).

1 I feel sick.
2 Hold my hand.
3 They've robbed the bank!
4 Can you tell me the time, please?
5 I'm going to lie down.

2 Complete the sentences with these words.

ill keep make remind travel

1 .... me to rent a DVD.
2 Can you .... a secret?
3 I'm going to .... a cake.
4 They're .... They've got fl u.
5 Does she .... a lot in her job?

3 Choose the correct option.

1 Come to my party! **Bring / Take** a friend!
2 Let's go for a walk. Let's **bring / take** the dogs.
3 Oh no, somebody's **robbed / stolen** my phone!
4 My house was **robbed / stolen** during the night.
5 Can you **lend / borrow** me a pencil?

Working on your own

4 Write translations of the words.

borrow / lend	lay / lie
come back / go back	raise / rise
do / make	recall / remind
hold / keep	rob / steal
ill / sick	say / tell
journey / travel / trip	

irregular nouns

The plural form of most nouns ends in *-s*. But some nouns are irregular.

people

children

1 Some plural nouns have irregular spelling. Choose the correct words.

1 How **much / many** people **live / lives** in your town?
2 **Is / Are** there a lot of children in your street?
3 There **is / are** three women and two men on the team.

2 Some nouns end in *-s*, but they are singular. Choose the correct words.

1 I think politics **seem / seems** interesting.
2 The news **was / were** surprising.
3 Maths **is / are** our first lesson on Monday.
4 **Is / Are** gymnastics your favourite sport?
5 Physics **isn't / aren't** easy for me.

3 Some nouns don't end in *-s*, but their verbs can be plural. Complete the sentences with these words.

bison committee family team police

1 Are .... the investigating the crime?
2 There aren't many wild .... in Europe.
3 Are your .... coming to see you?
4 The England .... aren't ready.
5 The .... are discussing the problem.

Working on your own

4 Write the plural form of these nouns.

bus country dish thief watch

5 Write your own sentence with each plural noun in Exercise 4.

8 Working with words

adjective → adverb

We can add *-ly* to some adjectives to make adverbs. (Note that not all words which end in *-ly* are adverbs.) There are some irregular adverbs which don't end in *-ly*.

1 Make adverbs from the adjectives in the table.

Adjective	Adverb	Adjective	Adverb
bad	badly	loud	....
calm	calmly	lucky	luckily
careful	....	patient	....
careless	....	quick	....
dangerous	....	quiet	....
easy	easily	safe	....
fast	fast	slow	....
hard	hard	well	well
late	late		

2 Complete the second sentence with an adverb from the table in Exercise 1.

1 Don't eat quickly. Eat ....!
2 Don't drive dangerously. Drive ....!
3 Don't talk loudly. Talk ....!
4 Don't work carelessly. Work ....!
5 Don't behave badly. Behave ....!

3 Choose the correct option.

1 We waited **patient / patiently** for the train.
2 We found the hotel **easy / easily**.
3 After the storm, the sea was **calm / calmly**.
4 The trip was **good / well**.
5 I don't speak French very **good / well**.

4 Complete the sentences with the adverbs. There is one extra adverb.

easily fast hard late luckily

1 The plane's going to arrive ....
2 This train goes ....!
3 I lost my ticket, but .... the travel agent gave me another one.
4 I've worked .... on my project.
5 I passed my exam ....

Working on your own

5 Choose five adverbs from the table in Exercise 1. Write your own sentence with each adverb.

verb + noun

There are some verbs and nouns that we often use together.

My dad drives a van at work.

I ride a bike to school.

1 Match these verbs and nouns. Then check your answers in the table.

climb drive fly ride sail

a camel a helicopter a lorry a mountain a ship

Verb	Noun
climb	a mountain, a wall
drive	a bus, a car, a lorry, a tractor, a taxi, a van
have	an accident, a health problem, a meal, a shower
fly	a helicopter, a micro-light, a plane
go	home, on holiday, shopping
play	a game, an instrument, a sport
ride	a bike, a camel, a horse
sail	a boat, a ship, a yacht
spend	money, time
take	a bus, a decision, medicine, a photo, a plane, a risk, a taxi, a train

2 Complete the sentences.

1 Do you often .... tennis?
2 How do you .... your free time?
3 Where did you .... on holiday?
4 Can you .... a horse?

3 Complete the sentences with the correct form of *have* or *take*.

1 I love .... photos.
2 I .... a painkiller when I had earache.
3 We .... an accident because we weren't careful.
4 You shouldn't .... risks in the sea.
5 I'm hungry. Let's .... lunch.

Working on your own

4 Choose five nouns from the table in Exercise 1. Write your own sentence with each noun.

VIDEO WORKSHEET

1 Monkey college

In Thailand, farmers use monkeys to pick coconuts from tall trees. The monkeys go to a special college to learn how to do this. It's a dangerous job for humans, but the coconut is an important fruit for Thai farmers. The monkeys are very valuable to the farmers and most people usually treat the monkeys well.

Before you watch

1 Read the introduction and discuss the questions.

1 What do the monkeys learn at college?
2 Why do you think picking coconuts is a dangerous job?

While you watch

PART ONE: The monkeys

2 Watch the first part of the film and choose the correct answer (a, b or c) for each question.

1 Who sends the monkeys to college?
  a Their parents.
  b Farmers.
  c The government.
2 What does the trainer use a rope for?
  a To help the monkey.
  b To catch the monkey.
  c To control and direct the monkey.
3 How do the monkeys pick the coconuts?
  a They twist the coconuts and they fall to the ground.
  b They take the coconuts in their hands.
  c They use the rope to make the coconuts fall to the ground.

3 Complete the sentences (1–3) with the words in the box below.

spin strategy pick

1 The monkeys learn how to .... coconuts from very tall trees.
2 It takes months for the young monkeys to learn the . for picking coconuts.
3 The monkeys learn how to .... a coconut in a box.

Watch again and check your answers.

PART TWO: Monkeys and people

4 Watch the second part of the film and choose the correct answer (a, b or c) for each question.

1 How many coconuts do farmers in Thailand produce each month?
  a Twenty thousand.
  b Two hundred thousand.
  c Two million.

5 Complete the sentences (1–3) with the words in the box below.

valuable lends earn

1 Farmers can .... about two dollars for every 100 coconuts that they sell.
2 Pak .... the monkey to other farmers to earn extra money.
3 The monkey is so .... that Pak never leaves it home alone.

Watch again and check your answers.

After you watch

6 Watch the whole film. Put the words in the correct order to make questions for the answers in bold.

1 is / School? / Training / Where / Monkey / the
In Surat Thani, Thailand.
2 trainer / month? / the / the / does / do / for / first / What
He lets the monkey play.
3 when / rope? / trainer / What / pulls / the / happens / the
The monkey goes faster.
4 the / monkeys / badly? / treat / Do / farmers
No, because the monkeys are important.

VIDEO WORKSHEET

2 Urban art

The works of two young urban artists – one musical, one visual – show us that urban art is all about innovation. A graffiti artist has an exhibition of his work at a traditional art gallery and a trumpeter mixes traditional jazz with modern hip hop music to create a new sound.

Before you watch

1 Read the introduction and discuss the questions.

1 Why do you think graffiti is 'urban art'?
2 What do you think 'innovative' means?

While you watch

PART ONE: The graffiti artist

2 Watch the first part of the film and choose the correct answer (a, b or c) for each question.

1 What is urban art is all about?
  a Respect for new work.
  b Art galleries.
  c Innovation.
2 What do real graffiti artists understand?
  a How to use only bright colours.
  b How to make their work distinctive.
  c How not to follow the rules.
3 Why does the gallery owner think that graffiti art is special?
  a Because it's always inventive.
  b Because it isn't pop art.
  c Because it doesn't sell well.

3 Complete the sentences (1–3) with the words in the box below.

cover	dimension	invites

1 It .... us to listen with new ears, and to look with new eyes.
2 In graffiti, you use colours that .... each other.
3 Graffiti art has brought a whole new .... to public art.

Watch again and check your answers.

PART TWO: The jazz musician

4 Watch the second part of the film and choose the correct answer (a, b or c) for each question.

1 What kind of music does Jafar Barron play?
  a Classical jazz.
  b Hip-hop and jazz.
  c A mix of jazz with rap and hip-hop.
2 What does art historian Donald Kimes say about what artists need to do?
  a Stay within their limits.
  b Build on their own cultural background.
  c Create a new cultural background.

5 Complete the sentences (1–3) with the words in the box below.

deal	respect	inventive

1 People are beginning to .... the talents of Jafar Barron.
2 His first CD is an .... mix of both worlds.
3 He also has a .... with a record company.

Watch again and check your answers.

After you watch

6 Watch the whole film. Put the words and phrases in the correct order to make sentences.

1 to use colour, / Real graffiti artists / work distinctive. / and how / to make their / understand how
2 in a / In the gallery, / enjoy / traditional setting. / the art / people can
3 has certainly / to public art. / new dimension / brought / Graffiti art / a whole
4 musicians. / parents / jazz / are / Both / his
5 of his / classical forms / own generation. / wanted to / Jafar / with / and hip-hop music / mix / more traditional, / the rap / of jazz

VIDEO WORKSHEET

3 Paraguay shaman

In the rainforests of Paraguay, there are many plants and herbs that can cure illness. However, the rainforests and the plants are disappearing. Scientists are working with traditional folk healers, called shamans, to learn and record all they can about these medicinal plants before the rainforests disappear.

Before you watch

1 Read the introduction and discuss the questions.

1 What is happening to the rainforests?

2 What do shamans know how to make from plants?

While you watch

PART ONE: The rainforests of Paraguay

2 Watch the first part of the film and choose the correct answer (a, b or c) for each question.

1 What is special about some of the plants and herbs in the rainforests of Paraguay?
- a You can use them to make medicine.
- b They are dangerous if you have malaria.
- c They cause fevers and colds.

2 What do the shamans have?
- a A deep knowledge of all areas of science.
- b A knowledge of local medicinal plants.
- c A big medical library.

3 Why is it a priority to record the shaman's knowledge about the rain forest plants?
- a Because there are so many trees in the rainforest.
- b Because the shaman is very old.
- c Because the rainforest is disappearing.

3 Complete the sentences (1–3) with the words and phrases in the box below.

diabetes   folk healer   medicinal

1 The rainforests have been a source of .... cures for a long time.

2 Traditional .... show us where to find the medicinal plants.

3 Paraguay has one of the highest .... rates in the world.

Watch again and check your answers.

PART TWO: The shaman

4 Watch the second part of the film and choose the correct answer (a, b or c) for each question.

1 How does shaman Gervasio prepare for the search for plants?
- a He prepares a special tea.
- b He uses chants and prayers.
- c He goes into the forest.

2 What are the scientists looking for?
- a A root called Suruvi.
- b A family of plants for cancer research.
- c Lots of different herbs and plants.

5 Complete the sentences (1–3) with the words and phrases in the box below.

published   spiritual connection   treat and cure

1 Gervasio uses chants and prayers to make a .... with the forest.

2 Suruvi is used to .... various illnesses.

3 Scientists have .... a book to help record and transmit Gervasio's knowledge.

Watch again and check your answers.

After you watch

6 Watch the whole film. Are the sentences true (T) or false (F)?

1 The rainforests of Paraguay have recently become a source of medicinal cures. **T / F**

2 Paraguay has one of the lowest rates of deforestation in the world. **T / F**

3 The traditional folk healers are called shamans. **T / F**

4 The shamans' knowledge is contained in big libraries of books. **T / F**

VIDEO WORKSHEET

4 Solar power

The sun is the most powerful source of energy on our planet, but it is difficult to store that energy for people to use. One town called Sacramento is very good at using solar energy and making it affordable. In the California desert, there is a very big solar generating plant, which can provide power for half a million people. It is a very clean source of energy.

Before you watch

1 Read the introduction and discuss the questions.

1 Why is it difficult for people to use the energy from the sun?

2 Why is the desert a good place for a solar power plant?

While you watch

PART ONE: A powerful source of energy

2 Watch the first part of the film and choose the correct answer (a, b or c) for each question.

1 What is the most powerful source of energy on our planet?

a The sun. **b** The moon. **c** Volcanoes.

2 What is important if we want to use solar as an alternative to other energy sources?

a It must be expensive.

b It must be reliable and people must be able to afford it.

c It must be more powerful than electricity.

3 What do many new homes in Sacramento have?

a Solar panels.

b No electricity.

c Solar cells.

3 Complete the sentences (1–3) with the words and phrases in the box below.

reduce   solar panels   sunlight

1 It's been difficult to turn that .... into electricity.

2 There are .... on many city buildings.

3 If you buy a lot of solar power at one time, it's possible to .... the price per unit.

Watch again and check your answers.

PART TWO: Kramer Solar Junction power facility

4 Watch the second part of the film and choose the correct answer (a, b or c) for each question.

1 What does net metering allow citizens to do with their extra solar power?

a Buy it. **b** Use it. **c** Sell it.

2 What is special about the Kramer Solar Junction power facility in California?

a It's the only solar plant in the U.S.

b It's very big.

c The technology is completely new.

5 Complete the sentences (1–3) with the words and phrases in the box below.

boiler   generator   tube

1 The mirrors reflect the sunlight onto a .... filled with special oil.

2 The 700-degree oil then goes into a .... that powers an electric turbine.

3 Each section also has a natural gas ....

Watch again and check your answers.

After you watch

6 Watch the whole film again. Are the sentences true (T) or false (F)?

1 More energy falls as sunlight on the U.S in a day than the U.S. uses in ten years. **T / F**

2 People can actually save or make money by buying a lot of solar power at one time. **T / F**

3 Net metering lets citizens sell energy back to the utility company. **T / F**

4 The Kramer Solar Junction power facility creates more energy than all the other solar panels in America put together.

VIDEO WORKSHEET

5 Man's best friend

Dogs help humans in many ways. Their strong sense of smell means they can help rescue people or find illegal drugs. We don't know exactly how or why the partnership between man and dog started. About 14,000 years ago, people began to work with wolves. Over time, the wolf became the intelligent domestic pet that is the dog today.

Before you watch

1 Read the introduction and discuss the questions.

1 Tell a partner about your dog or a dog you know.

2 Why is there a strong partnership between people and dogs?

While you watch

PART ONE: Working dogs

2 Watch the first part of the film and choose the correct answer (a, b or c) for each question.

1 What are dogs often known as?
- **a** Man's best pet.
- **b** Man's best friend.
- **c** Man's best partnership.

2 A dog's sense of smell is:
- **a** 10 times more powerful than our own.
- **b** 100 times more powerful than our own.
- **c** 1,000 times more powerful than our own.

3 What are some dogs trained to herd?
- **a** Livestock.
- **b** Blind people.
- **c** Huskies.

3 Complete the sentences (1–3) with the words in the box below.

blind	search	societies

1 Many .... have dogs as pets or rely on them to perform a variety of tasks.

2 Dogs use their powerful sense of smell to .... for people who are lost.

3 Dogs lead the .... and ease the lives of disabled people.

Watch again and check your answers.

PART TWO: Where dogs came from

4 Watch the second part of the film and choose the correct answer (a, b or c) for each question.

1 Why did humans acquire dogs?
- **a** Dogs and humans needed to protect each other from harm.
- **b** We still don't know.
- **c** It was a hunting partnership.

2 How long has the dog played an important role in human societies?
- **a** 14,000 years.
- **b** 1,4000 years.
- **c** 40,000 years.

5 Complete the sentences (1–3) with the words and phrases in the box below.

companionship	domestic pet	partnership

1 When did the remarkable .... between man and dog begin?

2 Over the years, the wolf became the talented .... we know today.

3 Was it the need for .... – a type of friendship?

Watch again and check your answers.

After you watch

6 Watch the whole film and answer the questions.

1 Which type of dog herds sheep?

2 Where do huskies work?

3 What is a 1,000 times more powerful than our own?

4 In what kinds of places can dogs use their sense of smell to search for humans?

5 Why are dogs used in airports?

6 When did the wolf begin working with people?

7 What is still unknown?

VIDEO WORKSHEET

6 The moon

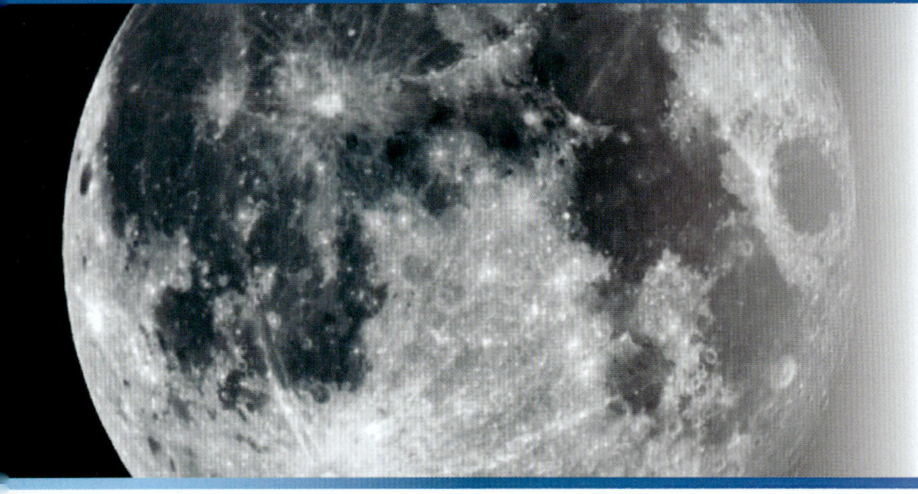

Scientists have studied the moon for hundreds of years. When man landed on the moon, it was one of the greatest advances in human history. The moon circles Earth in the same way as Earth goes round the sun. It has a powerful influence on our planet. The moon's gravity pulls the tides in our oceans which have helped shape Earth's coasts.

Before you watch

1 Read the introduction and discuss the questions.

1 What did Galileo use to look at the moon?

2 How long does it usually take for the moon to circle Earth?

While you watch

PART ONE: What is the moon?

2 Watch the first part of the film and choose the correct answer (a, b or c) for each question.

1 What did people once think the moon was made of?
- a Light.
- b Cheese.
- c Earth.

2 How do scientists think the moon was formed?
- a When an asteroid hit the earth.
- b When the earth hit an asteroid.
- c When the moon hit an asteroid.

3 Why does the moon have lots of holes or 'craters' on its surface?
- a Because it gets hit by lots of debris.
- b Because it has too much atmosphere.
- c Because it is so big.

3 Complete the sentences (1–3) with the words in the box below.

atmosphere cloud wonder

1 Since ancient times, the moon has been a cause of ....

2 The moon doesn't have much .... to protect it.

3 Eventually, this .... of rock and other material came together to form the moon.

Watch again and check your answers.

PART TWO : The moon and Earth

4 Watch the second part of the film and choose the correct answer (a, b or c) for each question.

1 What does the moon circle?
- a The sun.
- b The solar system.
- c The earth.

2 How many days does it take for the moon to complete its cycle?
- a 19.
- b 39.
- c 29.

5 Complete the sentences (1–3) with the words in the box below.

lunar gravity reflects

1 The moon has only one-sixth of the .... on Earth.

2 The moon .... light back from the sun.

3 When Earth comes exactly between the sun and a full moon, it creates a total .... eclipse.

Watch again and check your answers.

After you watch

6 Watch the whole film. Are the sentences true (T) or false (F)?

1 Some people thought the moon could turn people into strange beings called wolves. **T / F**

2 The moon is just one quarter the size of Earth. **T / F**

3 The first astronauts walked on the moon on July 20, 1969. **T / F**

4 The moon reflects light from Earth. **T / F**

5 The moon is full when it is on the far side of Earth. **T / F**

6 The moon does not have much effect on Earth. **T / F**

Inca mummy

In 1995, an archaeologist discovered the mummified body of an Inca girl preserved in ice in the Andes mountains in Peru. When he investigated more, he found some stone circles and more bodies of other children. Scientists believe that they were sacrifices to the gods. These mummified bodies are more evidence of the link between the ancient Incas and the Quechuan people who live in the area today.

Before you watch

1 Read the introduction and discuss the questions.

1 How did the Inca girl die?
2 Who are the Quechuan people?

While you watch

PART ONE: Juanita

2 Watch the first part of the film and choose the correct answer (a, b or c) for each question.

1 Where did the archaeologist Johan Reinhard discover the body of the girl?
  a At the top of a mountain.
  b In the jungle.
  c At the bottom of a mountain.

2 What did the Incas believe about the mountains?
  a The mountains divided the country in half.
  b The mountains were challenging.
  c The mountains were gods.

3 How did the Incas show respect for the gods?
  a By not living in the mountains.
  b By making offerings of young girls.
  c By making offerings of animals.

3 Complete the sentences (1–3) with the words in the box below.

offerings	descendants	mummified

1 The Quechuan people are believed to be direct .... of the Incas.
2 Parts of the body of the girl were ...., preserved in ice.
3 The Inca believed that if they made .... – in this case, young girls, the mountains would treat them well.

Watch again and check your answers.

PART TWO: Human sacrifice

4 Watch the second part of the film and choose the correct answer (a, b or c) for each question.

1 When Reinhard went back to conduct a second exploration, what did he find?
  a A stone circle and another body.
  b Six stone circles and two more bodies.
  c Rocks showing burial sites and lots of bodies.

2 Archaeologists believed that there were bodies at this site because:
  a It was a burial ground.
  b Lots of people died of cold there.
  c It was a site for human sacrifices.

5 Complete the sentences (1–3) with the words in the box below.

offerings	descendants	mummified

1 Circles of rock were used to show the location of b sites.
2 The discovery of more bodies implies that many people were s here.
3 The body was covered in c .

Watch again and check your answers.

After you watch

6 Watch the whole film again. Put the words and phrases in the correct order to make questions. Then answer the questions.

1 year / was the / made? / first discovery / In what
2 Why / a second / conduct / exploration? / did they
3 were found? / How / stone / circles / many
4 When was / the U.S.?/ body / sent to / the girl's
5 the American / What was / they sent / university / to? / the body / the name of
6 her injury? / did / How / find out about / the scientists

VIDEO WORKSHEET

8 Swimming with sharks

Diving with sharks is a popular tourist activity. To attract the sharks, tour guides give them food. People are worried that this will make sharks more likely to attack humans. This is why feeding wild animals is banned in all national parks in America and Canada. However, many people feel that diving with sharks helps them to understand sharks better and be less frightened of them.

Before you watch

1 Read the introduction and dicuss the questions.

1 Why is feeding sharks dangerous?
2 Why do people want to swim with sharks?

While you watch

PART ONE: Diving with sharks

2 Watch the first part of the film and choose the correct answer (a, b or c) for each question.

1 How is shark tourism described?
 a Big business.
 b Bad business.
 c Good business.

2 What do people no longer do?
 a Play with sharks.
 b Feed the sharks.
 c Swim with sharks.

3 Which animals are the least dangerous?
 a Sharks.
 b Bees.
 c Snakes.

3 Complete the sentences (1–3) with the words in the box below.

ban	foolish	horror

1 The .... of shark attack makes many people react against them.
2 Florida became the first state to .... the feeding of marine wildlife.
3 Some people think that it's .... to feed sharks and bring them close to busy beaches.

Watch again and check your answers.

PART TWO : Feeding the sharks

4 Watch the second part of the film and choose the correct answer (a, b or c) for each question.

1 What does the Marine Safety group want to ban?
 a Shark swimming.
 b Shark feeding.
 c Shark killing.

2 How often has shark feeding been associated with an attack on a human?
 a Never.
 b Occasionally.
 c Often.

5 Complete the sentences (1–3) with the words in the box below.

scary	strike	prey

1 You may not be a shark's .... , but sharks learn to associate humans with food.
2 When a shark does .... , it is usually 'hit and run.'
3 'I thought they'd be more ...., but they're not.'

Watch again and check your answers.

After you watch

6 Watch the whole film. Answer the questions.

1 How often does instructor Jeff Torode take customers to swim with sharks?
2 When did Florida become the first U.S. state to ban the feeding of marine wildlife?
3 What do dogs do more than sharks?
4 What do the numbers '60' and '3' refer to?
5 What greatly increases if you feed a wild animal?
6 For some divers, meeting sharks up close has what effect?

Grammar Explorer

Unit 1

present simple and verbs without a continuous form

We use the **present simple** to talk about:

- facts, general truths, laws of nature
  Paris is the capital of France.
  It snows in winter.
- permanent states
  My cousin lives in London.
- regular habits.
  I usually watch TV in the evening.
- feelings and thoughts
  I love playing rugby.
  I think this is a great school.

Affirmative						
I/You/We/You/They He/She/It	play … / like … / go … / etc. plays … / likes … / goes … / etc.					
Negative						
I/You/We/You/They He/She/It	don't (do not) doesn't (does not)	play … / like … / go … / etc.				
Questions						
Do Does	I/you/we/you/they he/she/it	play … / like … / go … / etc.?				
Short answers						
Yes,	I/you/ we/you/they	do.	No,	I/you/ we/you/they	don't.	
	he/she/it	does.		he/she/it	doesn't.	

Some verbs are called **stative** verbs because they describe a state, feeling or thought rather than an action. We DON'T normally use the present continuous with these verbs. They include:

> ***hate, know, like, love, need, prefer, seem, think, understand, want***
> ***I know what to do now.*** *[NOT I ~~am knowing~~ …]*
> ***The new student seems friendly.*** *[NOT The new student ~~is seeming~~ …]*
> ***I understand this exercise.*** *[NOT I ~~am understanding~~ …]*

present simple and present continuous

We use the **present simple** to talk about something that someone ***usually (often/always/etc.)*** does, or about a permanent state.

We use the **present continuous** to talk about actions that are in progress ***now***, at or around the time when we are talking, or about a temporary situation.

Fran usually lives in Rome.
She's living in Lisbon at the moment.

My dad works in a shop.
He isn't working today – it's Sunday.

Affirmative		
I'm You're/We're/You're/ They're He's/She's/It's	(I am) (You/We/You/ They are) (He/She/It is)	studying.
Negative		
I'm not You/We/You/They aren't He/She/It isn't	(I am not) (are not) (is not)	studying.
Questions		
Am Are Is	I you/we/you/they he/she/it	studying?

Short answers			
Yes,	I am. you/we/you/they are. he/she/it is.	No,	I'm not. you/we/you/they aren't. he/she/it isn't.

and, but, because, so

'Linking' words such as ***and***, ***but***, ***because*** and ***so*** are used to join two short sentences together into one longer sentence. The linking word shows a relationship between the main event/idea/etc. in each of the two short sentences. This relationship may be:

- **addition** (two similar events/ideas)
  He likes reading. He is interested in sports.
  (both sentences are about his likes/interests/etc.)
  He likes reading and (he) is interested in sports.
- **contrast** (two opposite events/ideas)
  I can speak Spanish. I can't speak French.
  (Sentence A is about ability; Sentence B is about inability)
  I can speak Spanish but I can't speak French.
- **cause/reason** (Sentence B gives the reason for Sentence A)
  I went to bed early. I was tired.
  (Sentence B explains why I went to bed early)
  I went to bed early because I was tired.
- **result** (Sentence B gives the result of Sentence A)
  I was tired. I went to bed early.
  (Sentence B explains the result of my feeling tired)
  I was tired so I went to bed early.

Unit 2

there was / there were

We use ***there was*** (with **singular or uncountable** nouns) and ***there were*** (with **plural** nouns) to describe what was in a place at a particular time in the past.

There was a jazz festival in my town last weekend. *[festival = singular]*

Grammar Explorer

***There was** some* really interesting **music**.* (*music = uncountable*)
***There were** some* great **groups** playing.* (*groups = plural*)

The negative form is ***there wasn't*** (singular and uncountable) and ***there weren't*** (plural).
***There wasn't** a **DJ** at the school party on Saturday.* (*DJ = singular*)
***There wasn't** any* **food**, either.* (*food = uncountable*)
***There weren't** any* **students** dancing.* (*students = plural*)

We make questions with ***Was there*** (singular and uncountable) and ***Were there*** (plural).
***Was there** a **cinema** in your town when you were a teenager, Gran?* (*cinema = singular*)
***Was there** any* other **entertainment**?* (*entertainment = uncountable*)
***Were there** any* **places** to go dancing?* (*places = plural*)

* Notice that with uncountable and plural nouns, we often use ***some*** in affirmative sentences, and ***any*** in negatives and questions.

Affirmative		
I You/We/You/They He/She/It	was were was	studying / dancing / etc.
Negative		
I wasn't (was not) You/We/You/They weren't (were not) He/She/It wasn't (was not)		studying / dancing / etc.
Questions		
Was Were Was	I you/we/you/they he/she/it	studying / dancing / etc.?

Short answers			
Yes,	I was. you/we/you/they were. he/she/it was.	No,	I wasn't. you/we/you/they weren't. he/she/it wasn't.

past simple and past continuous

We use the **past simple** to talk about:

- actions, events or states which started and finished in the past.
  We won the football match last Saturday.
- habits in the past, which are now finished.
  I played with my dolls every day when I was a little girl.
- a number of actions in the past which happened one after the other.
  He had a shower, put on his pyjamas and went to bed.

We use the **past continuous** to talk about actions that were in progress at a specific time in the past. We don't mention when the action started or finished.
We were playing football at 4 o'clock on Saturday afternoon.

Affirmative		
I/You/We You/They He/She/It	played ... / liked ... / went ... / etc.	
Negative		
I/You/We You/They He/She/It	didn't (did not)	play ... / like ... / go ... / etc.
Questions		
Did	I/you/we you/they he/she/it	play ... / like ... / go ... / etc.?

Short answers					
Yes,	I/you/we you/they he/she/it	did.	No,	I/you/we you/they he/she/it	didn't.

when, while and *during*

We use the **past continuous** for an action that was already in progress at the time a second, shorter action happened. We use the **past simple** for the action that happened second.
***They were walking home** (past continuous) **when it started to rain.** (past simple)*

We use ***when*** **+ past simple** OR ***while*** **+ past continuous** to talk about the two actions together.
***I was listening to music** (past continuous) **when my friend called.** (past simple)*
***My friend called** (past simple) **while I was listening to music.** (past continuous)*
We can put the two actions in any order, but we must still use ***when*** **+ past simple** OR ***while*** **+ past continuous**.
***When my friend called,** (past simple) **I was listening to music.** (past continuous)*
***While I was listening to music,** (past continuous) **my friend called.** (past simple)*

We use the **past simple** with ***during*** **+ noun phrase** to talk about actions that started and finished within a longer period of time in the past. We don't say exactly when the action happened. The noun phrase may state the period of time directly (e.g. *the 20th century, the last six months,* etc.) or refer to time indirectly (e.g. *my childhood, World War II,* etc.).
We can use ***during*** **+ noun phrase** at the beginning of a sentence or at the end.
***During the 1980s,** (noun phrase) **music videos became an important part of pop music.** (past simple)*
***He changed his style of singing** (past simple) **during the middle part of his career.** (noun phrase)*

present perfect

We use the **present perfect** to talk about:

- actions that happened in the past, at some time up to the

present, but exactly when the action happened is not known or not important.
***I've heard* this song before.** *(an hour ago? a week ago? a year ago?)*

- states that began in the past, but continue up to the present.
***She has been* a successful singer since she was a teenager.** *(she is still a successful singer now)*

We form the **present perfect** with ***have*** or ***has*** and the **past participle** of the main verb. With regular verbs, the past participle is the **bare infinitive** + ***-ed***.
We've** (have) **listened to lots of different types of music.
My favourite group has recorded a new album.

Irregular verbs do NOT form the past participle by adding ***-ed***. They have a different past participle form.
He's written a number of well-known pop songs.
Someone has broken my MP3 player!

Infinitive	Past	Past participle
be	was	been
come	came	come
do	did	done
get	got	got
go	went	gone
have	had	had
make	made	made
see	saw	seen

We form the negative with ***haven't*** or ***hasn't*** and the past participle of the main verb.
We make **present perfect** questions by putting ***Have/Has*** before the subject, and then the past participle of the main verb.
In short answers we use ***have/has*** or ***haven't/hasn't***. We DON'T use the main verb.

Affirmative					
I/You/We/You/They He/She/It		've (have) 's (has)		been ... / done ... / etc.	
Negative					
I/You/We/You/They He/She/It		haven't (have not) hasn't (has not)		been ... / done ... / etc.	
Questions					
Have Has		I/you/we/they he/she/it		(ever) been ... / done ... / etc.?	
Short answers					
Yes,	I/you/we/they he/she/it	have. has.	No,	I/you/we/they he/she/it	haven't. hasn't.

We can use the word ***ever*** in present perfect questions. It always goes before the main verb.
Have you ever been to a rock concert?
Has Coldplay ever performed in your country?

We can form negative sentences in the **present perfect** with the word ***never***. It always goes before the main verb.
I've never met a rock star.
Ben has never learned to play a musical instrument.

first, then, after, after that, before, during, in the end

'Linking' words/phrases such as ***first, then, after, after that, before, during*** and ***in the end*** are used to show the sequence of two or more actions/events – that is, the order in which they happened, or if they happened together.

- **first, then** and **after that** are used with two or more actions/events happening one after the other. We begin the sentence with the linking word/phrase, followed by **subject + verb**.
10 o'clock – We went shopping.
1 o'clock – We had lunch.
3 o'clock – We went to the cinema.
First we went shopping. Then we had lunch. After that, we went to the cinema.
- **before, during** and **after** compare the sequence of two actions or events. *Before* and *After* may be followed by a **noun phrase** OR **subject + verb**; *During* is followed only by a **noun phrase**. The main action/event – that is, the one we want to emphasise – is in the second part of the sentence.
10 o'clock – We went shopping.
1 o'clock – We had lunch (and decided what film to see).
3 o'clock – We went to the cinema.
Before we had lunch, we went shopping. During lunch, we decided what film to see. After lunch, we went to the cinema.
- **in the end** introduces an action or event which followed a series of actions/events already mentioned. It is followed by **subject + verb**, and suggests that what happened is not what was wanted/expected/etc.
Aneta wanted to see a thriller. I wanted to see a musical. In the end, we saw a comedy.

Unit 3

present perfect with *yet, already* and *just*

We can use the word ***yet*** with the **present perfect** in questions and negative sentences. It always goes at the end of the sentence.
We often use ***yet*** when we expect that something has either just/already happened or, if not, that it will happen soon.
- Have you finished your homework yet?
- No, I haven't finished yet. I'll do it this evening.

We use the word ***already*** with the **present perfect** in affirmative sentences. It usually goes between *have/has* and the main verb. We often use ***already*** when something has happened sooner than we expected.

Grammar Explorer

- *Have you finished your homework?*
- *Yes – and I've already done my project for Friday, too!*

We usually use the word ***just*** with the **present perfect** in affirmative sentences. It always goes between *have/has* and the main verb.
We use ***just*** to show that something happened a very short time ago.
- *Have you finished your homework?*
- *Finished? I've just started!*

present perfect with *for* and *since*

We use the word ***for*** with the **present perfect** to talk about *duration* – that is, how long it has been from the start of a state or situation until now.
For is followed by a phrase that describes a period of time.
She has been a medical student for three years.

We use the word ***since*** with the **present perfect** for a state or situation which has continued up to the present, to talk about when it started.
Since is followed by a time/day/year/etc., or a phrase that describes a particular time.
Mark has been a doctor since 2007.
I have hated hospitals since I was a young child.

present perfect and past simple

We use the **present perfect** to talk about something happening during a period of time that started in the past and goes up to the present. This includes:

- a state that continues up to the present
  Aneta has lived in England for eight years. *(She still lives there.)*
- an action that has been repeated a number of times and may be repeated again in the future
  Lauren has been to Ireland several times. *(She may go there again.)*

We use the **past simple** to talk about completed action at a finished time in the past. We use this when:

- we say or understand when the action happened
  Aneta's family moved to England when she was seven.
  Lauren went to Ireland again last month.
- we know that the period of time in which it happened is completely in the past and does not continue up to the present
  Shakespeare wrote many famous plays. *(He died about 400 years ago.)*

so / neither + auxiliary verb or *be* + subject

We use ***so*** and ***neither*** to show that a statement which has just been made about one subject (a person/group/thing/etc.) is also true for another subject.
This often happens when someone makes a statement about their own feelings, experiences etc., and another person agrees that they also have/had the same feeling or experience.

We use ***so*** to agree with an affirmative statement, and ***neither*** to agree with a negative statement.
A: I was really scared during that movie!
B: So was I.

A: I haven't done my homework yet.
B: Neither have I.

The pattern is ***So / Neither*** **+ modal / auxiliary /** ***be*** **+ subject**.
We use the same modal (*can, must, will,* etc.), auxiliary (*do/does/did, have/has/had*) or form of *be* as in the first statement.
Jack can ride a bike. So can Lee.
Lauren has been abroad several times. So has Jack.
Spain is a country in Europe. So is France.

If the first statement is negative, we use the same modal, auxiliary or form of *be* in the second statement, but not in the negative form, because *neither* is already negative.
You can't speak Chinese. Neither can~~'t~~ we.
She doesn't like sports. Neither does~~n't~~ he.

If the first statement doesn't have a modal, auxiliary or *be,* then we use *do/does* or *did*.
Aneta loves reading. So does Lee.
Aneta felt unwell when she had sunstroke. So did Jack.

Another way to agree with another person's statement is to use ***Me too*** and ***Me neither***. ***Me too*** agrees with an *affirmative statement*, and ***Me neither*** agrees with a *negative statement*. This is the same for all modals, auxiliaries and forms of *be,* in any tense.
A: I was really scared during that movie!
B: Me too.

A: I haven't done my homework yet.
B: Me neither.

When someone makes a statement about their own feelings, experiences etc., another person might disagree – that is, they might say that they do/did not have the same feeling or experience.
In this case, we can use **subject + modal / auxiliary /** ***be***.
Notice that we use the same modal, auxiliary or form of *be* in the second statement, but IN THE OPPOSITE FORM – in other words, if the first statement is affirmative, we use the negative form in the second statement; if the first statement is negative, we use the affirmative form in the second statement.
A: I was really scared during that movie!
B: I wasn't.

A: I haven't done my homework yet.
B: I have.

although, even though, however

The 'linking' words/phrases ***Although, Even though*** and ***However*** are used to show that two actions/events/states/etc. are opposite in some way.

- **although** and **even though** show that the second action/event/etc. is the opposite of what we would expect to follow the first action/event/etc. **Although** and **even though** join the two actions/events/etc. into one sentence.

Lee wasn't feeling well. (We would expect him to stay in bed.)
He went to the party. (The opposite of what we would expect.)
***Although** Lee wasn't feeling well, he went to the party.*
*Lee went to the party, **even though** he wasn't feeling well.*

Notice that we normally use ***although*** at the beginning of the sentence, followed by the first action/event/state etc., and the unexpected action/event/etc. is in the second part of the sentence. With ***even though***, we normally put the unexpected action/event/etc. at the beginning of the sentence.

- **however** begins a sentence about the opposite action/ event/etc. It shows the contrast between the two actions/ events/etc., but it does not join them into one sentence. **However** is followed by a comma.
  I can speak Spanish. I can't speak French.
  I can speak Spanish. However, I can't speak French.

Unit 4

passive

In the active voice, the subject of the sentence is the person/ group/thing/etc. that does or causes the action. When we use the **passive**, the subject is the person/group/thing/etc. that the action happens to. That is, the object of a sentence in the active voice becomes the subject of the sentence in the **passive**.

SUBJECT	VERB	OBJECT	
Greenhouse gases	***cause***	***global warming.***	(Active)
Global warming	***is caused***	***by greenhouse gases.***	(Passive)
SUBJECT	VERB	AGENT	

We form the **passive** with ***be*** **+ past participle** of the verb in the active sentence. The tense of *be* is the same as the tense of the verb in the active sentence.

Global warming affects weather patterns. *(present simple)*
Weather patterns are affected by global warming.

An earthquake caused the tsunami. *(past simple)*
The tsunami was caused by an earthquake.

We form the negative with ***isn't/aren't*** **+ past participle** in the present simple, and ***wasn't/weren't*** **+ past participle** in the past simple.
The cause of this environmental problem still isn't known.
Scientists' warnings about the problem weren't taken seriously until recently.

We form questions by putting ***Is/Are*** or ***Was/Were*** before the subject, and then the past participle of the main verb.
Are wild animals protected against the dangers of pollution?

We can use **question words** such as ***What***, ***Why***, ***Where***, ***How*** etc. to ask for extra information rather than a simple 'Yes' or 'No' answer.
How many rainforest trees are cut down every minute?
When was solar energy used for the first time?

We use the **passive** when we want to emphasise the subject and/or the action itself. If we want to say who/what does the action (the 'agent'), we use *by*. If it is not important or not clear who the agent is (e.g. *someone, they, people,* etc.), then we don't include it.
People waste millions of litres of water every day. *(Active)*
Millions of litres of water are wasted ~~by people~~ every day. *(Passive)*
They showed the volcanic eruption on TV. *(Active)*
The volcanic eruption was shown ~~by them~~ on TV. *(Passive)*

many, much, few, little

We use ***many*** and ***few*** with countable nouns, and ***much*** and ***little*** with uncountable nouns.

Few means 'not many', and ***little*** means 'not much'.

We normally use ***many*** and ***much*** only in questions and negative sentences. In affirmative sentences, we use ***lots of / a lot of*** instead.

There are few pandas** (countable) **still living in their natural environment. Not much effort** (uncountable) **was made to help them until it was almost too late, and not many of these animals** (countable) **have survived. Even now, there is little hope** (uncountable) **that the situation will improve. A lot of the bamboo forests** (countable) **where the pandas once lived were destroyed. Conservationists have shown a lot of interest** (uncountable) **in solving the problem – but how many years** (countable) **will it take, and how much time** (uncountable) **is left before this species disappears?

for example, such as, including, also, too

The linking words/phrases ***for example***, ***such as*** and ***including*** are used to introduce examples of something mentioned in the previous sentence, or in the first part of the same sentence.

The linking words ***also*** and ***too*** are used to show that something is similar to what was mentioned in the previous sentence.

- **For example** is used at the beginning of a new sentence. It is followed by a comma, then **subject + verb.**
  Wild animals face many dangers. For example, they may be threatened by hunting and destruction of their habitat.
- **such as** and **including** join the example(s) to the first part of the sentence, and they are followed by **nouns** or **noun phrases**.
  Wild animals face many dangers, such as / including hunting and destruction of their habitat.
- ***also*** and ***too*** show the similarity between the ideas in two sentences, but they do not join them into one sentence. ***Also*** comes immediately before the main verb, or after the verb *be*. ***Too*** is normally used at the end of the sentence.
  Global warming may cause sea levels to rise. It may also cause changes in weather patterns.
  Global warming may cause sea levels to rise. It may cause changes in weather patterns too.

Grammar Explorer

Unit 5

permission and obligation

Permission and obligation are about what the law, school or club rules, our parents, etc. tell us to do.

Permission is about things we <u>want</u> to do; laws, rules, parents, etc. tell us which of these things we ***can*** do, and which of these things we ***can't*** do.

- **can**
  Can has the same form for all subjects and is followed by the **bare infinitive**. The negative is ***can't*** (***cannot***) and it is the same for all subjects. The past form is ***could***.
  We can wear ordinary clothes at school.
  We can't wear makeup at school, though.

Affirmative		
I/You/He/She/It/ We/You/They	can	wear ... / do ... / etc.
Negative		
I/You/He/She/It/ We/You/They	can't (cannot)	wear ... / do ... / etc.
Questions		
Can	I/you/he/she/it/we/you/they	wear ... / do ... / etc.?
Short answers		
Yes, No,	I/you/he/she/it/we/you/they	can. can't.

- **let**
  If you ***let*** someone do something, you give them permission to do it. The affirmative is ***let/lets*** **+ object + bare infinitive**.
  Let is a full verb, and we form the negative and questions in the same way as normal verbs.
  Let can <u>not</u> be used in the passive.
  My mum lets me wear lipstick and nail varnish when I go out.
  My parents don't let me stay out late.
  Does your dad let you use his computer?

- **allow**
  Allow has the same meaning as ***let***, but the affirmative is ***allow/allows*** **+ object +** **<u>full</u> infinitive**. ***Allow*** is a full verb, and we form the negative and questions in the same way as normal verbs.
  Allow <u>can</u> be used in the passive.
  The school doesn't allow us <u>to</u> go home at lunchtime.
  Does the law allow a 16-year-old <u>to</u> ride a motorbike?

- **be allowed**
  If laws/rules/etc. *allow* you to do something, you ***are allowed to*** do it. In other words, ***be allowed*** is the passive of *allow* and it is followed by the **<u>full</u> infinitive**.
  We aren't allowed <u>to</u> wear jeans at school.

Obligation is mainly about things we <u>don't want</u> to do; laws, rules, parents, etc. tell us which of these things we ***must*** do, and which things we ***mustn't*** do.

- **must**
  Must has the same form for all subjects and is followed by the **bare infinitive**. The negative is ***mustn't*** (***must not***) and it is the same for all subjects. The past form is ***had to****.
  Students must be quiet in the classroom.
  Students mustn't talk during an exam.

Affirmative		
I/You/He/She/It/ We/You/They	must	wear ... / do ... / etc.
Negative		
I/You/He/She/It/ We/You/They	mustn't (must not)	wear ... / do ... / etc.
Questions		
Must	I/you/he/she/it/ we/you/they	wear ... / do ... / etc.?
Short answers		
Yes, No,	I/you/he/she/it/we/you/they	must. don't have to.**

- **have to**
  We use ***have to*** to talk about what is necessary – because of a rule/law/etc., or because of the situation.
  We form the affirmative with ***have/has to*** **+ bare infinitive**.
  The past form is ***had to****.
  We have to wear a horrible school uniform.
  We make questions by putting ***Do/Does*** before the subject, and then ***have to*** **+ bare infinitive**.
  Do I have to tidy my room?

Affirmative			
I/You/We/You/They He/She/It	have to has to	wear ... / do ... / etc.	
Negative			
I/You/We/You/They He/She/It	don't have to doesn't have to	wear ... / do ... / etc.	
Questions			
Do Does	I/you/we/you they/he/she/it	have to	wear ... / do ... / etc.?

Short answers					
Yes,	I/you/we/you they/he/she/it	do. does.	No,	I/you/we/you they/he/she/it	don't. doesn't.

- **make**
  If you ***make*** someone do something, you give them an order and so they do it, although they don't want to. The

affirmative is ***make/makes* + object + <u>bare</u> infinitive**. *Make* is a full verb, and we form the negative and questions in the same way as normal verbs.
Make <u>can</u> be used in the passive.
Our mum always makes us help with the housework.
Do your teachers make you do a lot of homework?

- **be made**
  If somebody *makes* you do something, you ***are made to*** do it. In other words, ***be made*** is the passive of *make*.
  But be careful:
  make is followed by the **<u>bare</u> infinitive.**
  be made is followed by the **<u>full</u> infinitive**.
  The boy who broke the window was made <u>to</u> pay to fix it.

No obligation means that there isn't a rule/person/etc. telling you to do this thing.

- **don't have to**
  If you ***don't have to*** do something, it means it isn't necessary to do it. (but you can do it if you want to).
  I don't have to go to bed early on Fridays and Saturdays.

* ***Must*** and ***have to*** mean the same thing, and the past form of ***must*** is ***had to***.
But be careful:
**** *mustn't*** does <u>not</u> mean *don't have to*. It means *not allowed to*.
You don't have to cycle to school – you can walk. *[It's not necessary.]*
You mustn't cycle on the walkway. *[You're not allowed to.]*

reflexive pronouns and *each other*

We use ***each other*** when person A does something (e.g. *looks at, talks to*, etc.) to person B, and person B does the same thing to person A.
Aneta looked at Jack, and Jack looked at Aneta.
= Aneta and Jack looked at each other.
My pen friend often writes to me, and I often write to my pen friend.
= My pen friend and I often write to each other.

We use **reflexive pronouns** (***myself***, ***yourself***, etc.) with verbs such as *burn, cut, hurt, kill, look at, teach*, etc. when the same person is both the subject <u>and</u> the object of the verb.
Steve *(subject)* ***cut himself*** *(i.e. Steve – object)* ***while he was preparing dinner.***
Did you *(subject)* ***hurt yourself*** *(i.e. you – object)* ***when you fell off your bike?***
I *(subject)* ***taught myself*** *(i.e. me – object)* ***to play the guitar.***

Subject pronouns							
I	you	he	she	it	we	you	they

Reflexive pronouns
myself yourself himself herself itself ourselves yourselves themselves

relative pronouns and relative clauses

We use a **relative clause** to give extra information about the main part of a sentence. Often the meaning of the main part of the sentence is not complete without this information.
There is the man.
(What man? The meaning of the sentence is not complete.)

The extra information contains a pronoun or adverb which <u>relates to</u> a noun in the main part of the sentence.
He stole your car.
(The pronoun 'he' relates to the noun 'man' in the first sentence.)

We join the two parts of the sentence by changing the pronoun or adverb into a **relative pronoun** (*who, which*) or **relative adverb** (*when, where*) and placing it after the noun it relates to, followed by the rest of the relative clause.
We use:

- ***who*** for **people**
- ***which*** for **things**
- ***when*** for **times**
- ***where*** for **places**

There is the man <u>who</u> <u>stole your car</u>.
(The relative pronoun 'who' goes after the noun it relates to, followed by the rest of the relative clause.)

Placing the relative pronoun or relative adverb after the noun it relates to may involve changing the word order.
Summer is the time.
(What time? The meaning of the sentence is not complete.)
Most people go on holiday then.
(The adverb 'then' relates to the noun 'time' in the first sentence.)
Summer is the time <u>when</u> <u>most people go on holiday</u>.
(The relative adverb 'when' goes after the noun it relates to, followed by the rest of the relative clause.)

The relative clause may sometimes be in the middle of the main part of the sentence, rather than at the end.
The dog is standing over there.
It bit me.
(The pronoun 'it' relates to the noun 'dog'.)
The dog <u>which</u> <u>bit me</u> is standing over there.
(The relative pronoun 'which' goes after the noun it relates to, followed by the rest of the relative clause, and so the relative clause is in the middle of the main clause.)

The park is at the end of this street.
Jake and Lauren play tennis there.
(The adverb 'there' relates to the noun 'park'.)
The park <u>where</u> <u>Jake and Lauren play tennis</u> is at the end of this street.
(The relative adverb 'where' goes after the noun it relates to, and the relative clause is in the middle of the main clause.)

In this type of relative clause, we can also use ***that*** instead of *who* or *which*.
There is the man that stole your car.
The dog that bit me is standing over there.

Grammar Explorer

both and *neither*

We use ***both*** and ***neither*** to show that two people, groups, things, etc. are the same in some way.

We use ***both of*** + **object pronoun** in an affirmative statement.
Lauren plays tennis. Jack also plays tennis.
= ***Both of them play* tennis.***

We use ***neither of*** + **object pronoun** in a negative statement.
You aren't interested in fashion. I'm not interested in fashion, either.
= ***Neither of us is* interested in fashion.***

* Notice that ***both*** takes a verb in the **plural**, but ***neither*** takes a verb in the **singular**.

We can use several patterns with ***both***:

- *both of* + object pronoun + verb
  Both of them play tennis.
- subject pronoun + *be* + *both*
  They are both good tennis players.
- subject pronoun + modal/auxiliary + *both* + main verb
  They have both played tennis since they were young.
- subject pronoun + *both* + main verb
  They both play tennis in the park.

Unit 6

first conditional

We use the **first conditional** to talk about future actions or predictions which depend on a *condition* – that is, another (usually future) event where two things are possible.

Will it be hot tomorrow? → YES → We'll go to the beach.
Will it be hot tomorrow? → NO → We'll go to the cinema.

Each of the different possibilities in the condition will cause a different result in the future.
If it is hot tomorrow, we'll go to the beach.
If it isn't hot tomorrow, we'll go to the cinema.

> We form the **first conditional** with ***If*** + **present simple** for the condition, followed by a **future** form for the resulting future action or prediction. We do NOT use a future form for the condition.
> ***If it rains*** (NOT ~~If it will rain~~) ***tomorrow, I'll take an umbrella.***
> ***If they feel*** (NOT ~~If they will feel~~) ***tired, they won't go to the cinema.***
> ***If you don't take*** (NOT ~~If you won't take~~) ***a map, you'll get lost.***

The future form we use most often is ***will/won't*** + **bare infinitive**, but this is not the only future form we use. We also use the future form of ***can*** (i.e. ***will be able to*** + **bare infinitive**) and ***must*** (i.e. ***will have to*** + **bare infinitive**).
If it rains tomorrow, we won't be able to go for a picnic.
If we plan to reach London before lunchtime, we will have to leave very early in the morning.

predicting

We can use ***will***, ***may*** and ***might*** to talk about predictions about the future.

Will, ***may*** and ***might*** have the same form for all subjects *(I, you, he,* etc.*)*. The main verb after these modals is in the **bare infinitive**.
One day we will send astronauts to Mars.
They may find signs of life there.
Our great-grandchildren might even go to live on Mars!

The negative of ***will*** is ***won't*** *(**will not**)* and it is the same for all subjects. The negative of ***may*** and ***might*** is ***may not*** and ***might not***, and these are also the same for all subjects.

Will usually suggests we are quite sure about our prediction, ***may*** suggests we are not so sure, and ***might*** usually suggests we are even less sure. We often use these modals after *I think, I'm sure,* etc., and/or with words such as *probably, perhaps, certainly,* etc., to show more clearly how sure we are about our prediction.
I'm sure scientists will find a cure for most diseases soon.
I think it may be hot tomorrow.
People might possibly live on the Moon in 2110.

going to for plans and intentions

We use ***be going to*** about the future when we have already decided what to do, and have made some plans.
This may include informal plans about the near future, or plans about our ambitions for something in the distant future.
I'm going to go to university next year. I'm going to study medicine.
The government says it's going to reduce pollution levels.
Lauren's going to play hockey with the school team this afternoon.

We form the **affirmative** with ***am/are/is*** + ***going to*** + the **bare infinitive** of the main verb.
We form the **negative** with ***am/are/is*** + ***not*** + ***going to*** + the **bare infinitive** of the main verb.
We make **questions** by putting ***am/are/is*** before the subject, and then ***going to*** + the **bare infinitive** of the main verb.
In **short answers** we use ***am/'m not***, ***are/aren't*** or ***is/isn't***. We DON'T use the main verb.

> Be careful with ***be going*** (*present continuous*) and ***be going to go***.
> ***I'm going to Jack's house – come with me!*** (*present continuous*)
> ***I'm going to go to university next year. (be going to)***

Affirmative			
I'm You're/We're/ You're/They're He's/She's/It's	(I am) (You/We/ You/They are) (He/She/It is)	going to	go ... / be ... / etc.
Negative			
I'm not You/We/ You/They aren't He/She/It isn't	(I am not) (You/We/You/ They are not) (He/She/It is not)	going to	go ... / be ... / etc.

Questions			
Am Are Is	I you/we/ you/they he/she/it	going to	go ... / be ... / etc.?

Short answers			
Yes,	I am. you/we/you/they are. he/she/it is.	No,	I'm not. you/we/you/they aren't. he/she/it isn't.

so that and *in order to*

We use ***so that*** and ***in order to*** at the beginning of clauses of purpose – that is, the part of a sentence which explains why somebody does/did something.

We form clauses of purpose with:
- ***so that*** + subject + can/could* + bare infinitive
- ***in order to*** + bare infinitive

I must buy a camera so that I can take photos when I'm on holiday.
My dad always cycles to work in order to keep fit.

** We can also use* be, *but this is the most common pattern.*

Unit 7

reporting verbs

Direct speech gives the exact words someone said and uses quotation marks ('...') to show this.
'I like living in Britain,' Daisy said. *(Direct speech)*
Reported speech gives the meaning of what somebody said, but doesn't use their exact words and doesn't use quotation marks. For example, we use reported speech when we tell somebody else what another person said.
Daisy said that she likes living in Britain. *(Reported speech)*

In **direct speech**, the exact words someone uses can show us if they are speaking (e.g.) politely, angrily, etc. In **reported speech**, where we don't use their exact words, we can use different **reporting verbs** to show this sort of information.

Direct speech	Reported speech
'Sit down – now!' she shouted.	***She ordered me to sit down.***
'Sit down,' she said.	***She told me to sit down.***
'Sit down, please,' she said.	***She asked me to sit down.***
'Would you like to sit down?' she said.	***She invited me to sit down.***

Reporting verbs we use in this way include:
advise ask invite order remind tell warn

The normal pattern is **verb + object (+ not) + full infinitive**
The teacher told her students (not) to open their books.
But: we usually don't *invite* someone not to do something
we usually only *warn* someone not to do something

word order in indirect questions

We can make a statement into a **direct question** by putting a modal, auxiliary or *be* before the subject. If the statement does not have a modal, auxiliary or *be*, we add *do/does/did* before the subject.

Statement	Direct question
Jack can play the violin.	***Can Jack play the violin?***
Daisy is from America.	***Is Daisy from America?***
Lee loves reading.	***Does Lee love reading?***

We can also make **direct questions** beginning with **question words** such as ***What***, ***When***, ***How***, etc. Again, we put a modal, auxiliary or *be* before the subject, and if the statement does not have a modal, auxiliary or *be*, we add *do/does/did* before the subject.

Direct question	Question with question word
Can Jack play the violin?	***What can Jack play?***
Is Daisy from America?	***Where is Daisy from?***
Does Lee love reading?	***What does Lee love doing?***

If we add a phrase such as *I don't know*, *I'm not sure* or *I wonder* in front of the question, then it becomes an **indirect question** and the word order goes back to the word order of statements – that is, **subject + modal/auxiliary** (if there is one) **+ verb**.

Direct question	Indirect question
What can Jack play?	***I don't know what Jack can play.***
Where is Daisy from?	***I'm not sure where Daisy is from.***
What does Lee love doing?	***I wonder what Lee loves doing.***

If the **direct question** does not begin with a question word, we use the word ***if***. Again, the word order goes back to the word order of statements.

Can Jack play the violin? *(Direct question)*
I don't know if Jack can play the violin. *(Indirect question)*

Is Daisy from America? *(Direct question)*
I'm not sure if Daisy is from America. *(Indirect question)*

Does Lee love reading? *(Direct question)*
I wonder if Lee loves reading. *(Indirect question)*

Grammar Explorer

We can make a **direct question** more polite by beginning with a phrase such as *Can/Could you tell me ... ?* or *Do you know ... ?* The original question is now an **indirect question**, and the word order goes back to the word order of statements. The indirect question begins with a question word or ***if***.

Where is the lecture hall? *(Direct question)*
Do you know where the lecture hall is? *(Indirect question)*

How much does this cost? *(Direct question)*
Can you tell me how much this costs? *(Indirect question)*

Is this my seat? *(Direct question)*
Could you tell me if this is my seat? *(Indirect question)*

Unit 8

second conditional

We use the **second conditional** to talk about imaginary actions or results which depend on an imaginary condition – not a real condition – in the present or future.

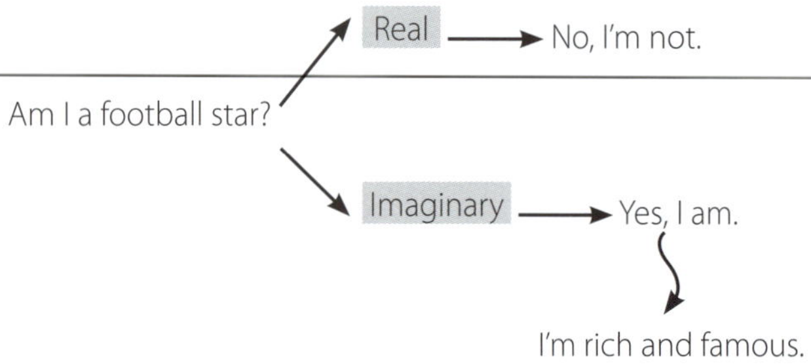

If I was a football star, I'd be rich and famous.

> We form the **second conditional** with ***If*** **+ past simple** for the condition, followed by ***would /wouldn't*** **+ bare infinitive** for the resulting action or situation. We do NOT use ***would*** for the condition.
>
> We can put the two parts of the sentence in any order.
> ***If I was lost in the jungle*** (condition), ***I'd try not to panic*** (result).
> ***I wouldn't be frightened*** (result) ***if I saw a shark*** (condition).
>
> Notice that the use of the **past simple** in the condition does NOT show completed action – it shows 'not real'.
> ***If*** **+ past simple** = imaginary ('unreal') in the present/ future.

Would has the same form for all subjects and is followed by the **bare infinitive**. In the affirmative, we almost always use the short form (*I'd, You'd, He'd, She'd,* etc.). The negative of ***would*** is ***wouldn't*** (***would not***).

We make questions by putting ***would*** before the subject, and then the **bare infinitive** of the main verb. In short answers we use ***would*** or ***wouldn't***. We DON'T use the main verb.
We can also make questions using **question words**.
What would you do if you saw a snake?

Affirmative		
I/You/He/She/It/We/You/They	'd (would)	be ... / go ... / etc.
Negative		
I/You/He/She/It/We/You/They	wouldn't (would not)	be ... / go ... / etc.
Questions		
Would	I/you/he/she/it/we/you/they	be ... / go ... / etc.?
Short answers		
Yes, No,	I/you/he/she/it/we/you/they I/you/he/she/it/we/you/they	would. wouldn't.

We use ***would*** for:

- the result clause in second conditional sentences
  If you won €1 million, what would you do with it?
- polite offers & invitations
  Would you like me to help you?
- polite requests
  I'd like a double cheeseburger and large chips, please.
- giving advice
  If I was/were you, I wouldn't do that.

quantifiers + adjectives

We use an adjective to say that something is, for example, *difficult* – but this does not say how difficult it is.
We can add a 'modifier' such as ***very***, ***really***, ***quite***, etc. to the adjective to give this extra information. For example:
Learning English is quite difficult, but learning Chinese is very difficult.

- ***very***, ***really***, ***quite***, ***a bit*** **+ adjective**

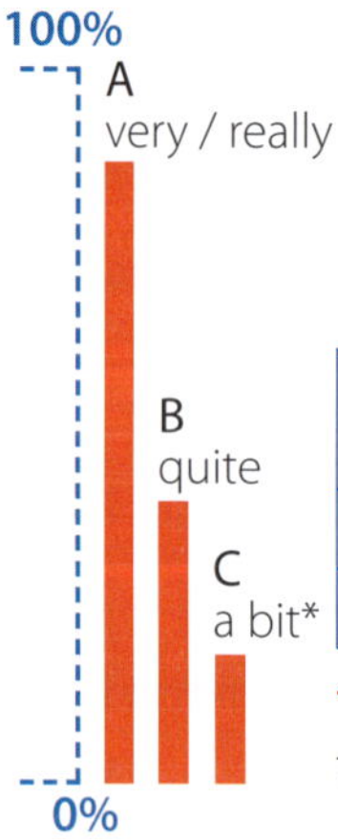

A is	very really	easy	safe	exciting	etc.
B is	quite	difficult*	dangerous*	boring*	etc.
C is	a bit*				

* ***a bit*** **+ adjective** is used only with adjectives that suggest a negative feeling.

- ***much***, ***a lot***, ***a bit*** + **comparative adjective** (*-er, more/less*)

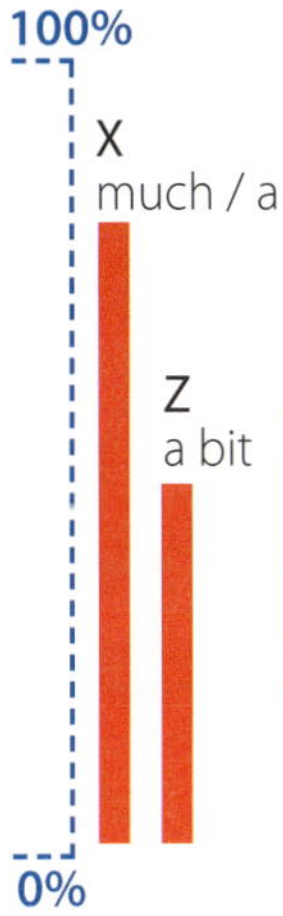

X is	much	easier	more difficult	
	a lot	safer	more dangerous	etc.
Z is	a bit*	more exciting	more boring	

* ***a bit*** + **comparative adjective** is used with all adjectives – i.e. adjectives that suggest a negative or a positive feeling.

unless, in case and *or*

Unless, ***in case*** and ***or*** are used in sentences which are kinds of first conditional.

We have seen the most common pattern of the **first conditional** which is:

If + present ... future

If it rains tomorrow, we won't go to the beach.

- ***Unless*** follows this common pattern, but it means **if + negative**:
  You'll miss your train ***if*** you ***don't*** hurry.
  = ***You'll miss your train unless you hurry.***

However, there is another common first conditional pattern, which is:

If + present ... imperative

The **imperative** is a command, such as 'Come here!' or 'Sit down!' Its form is the same as the bare infinitive, but it has no subject. In a conditional sentence, it takes the place of the ... *future* clause.

If you need help, call me.

- ***In case*** means *'because this might **happen**'*. It usually follows the imperative, so it goes in the place of the ***if + present simple*** clause:
  Take your umbrella ***because*** it ***might*** rain.
  = ***Take your umbrella in case it rains.*** [NOT *in case it ~~will rain~~*]
- ***Or*** means *'if the opposite **happens**'*. It usually follows the imperative, but it removes the whole *If + present simple* clause, so it is followed by ***... future***. An easy way to remember this is that ***or*** joins two similar things; in a conditional sentence, the imperative is similar to the ... *future* clause.
  Be careful. ***If you aren't careful***, you'll hurt yourself.
  = ***Be careful or you'll hurt yourself.***

future	...	***unless + present simple***
imperative	...	***in case + present simple***
imperative	...	***or + future***

NATIONAL GEOGRAPHIC LEARNING | CENGAGE Learning

English Explorer Student's Book 3
Helen Stephenson
Jane Bailey

Publisher: Jason Mann

Adaptations Manager: Alistair Baxter

Assistant Editor: Manuela Barros

Technology Development Manager: Debie Mirtle

Product and Marketing Manager: Ruth McAleavey

Senior Content Project Editor: Natalie Griffith

Senior Production Controller: Paul Herbert

National Geographic Liaison: Leila Hishmeh

Art Director: Natasa Arsenidou

Cover/Text Designer: Natasa Arsenidou

Compositors: Ioanna Ioannidou & Sophia Ioannidou

Audio: EFS Television Production Ltd

Acknowledgements

The publisher would like to thank Robert Crossley for writing the True Story and Project pages.

The Publisher would also like to thank the following for their invaluable contribution: Nick Sheard, Karen Spiller and Liz Driscoll.

ISBN: 978-1-111-06798-4

National Geographic Learning
Cheriton House, North Way, Andover, Hampshire, SP10 5BE
United Kingdom

Cengage Learning is a leading provider of customized learning solutions with office locations around the globe, including Singapore, the United Kingdom, Australia, Mexico, Brazil and Japan. Locate your local office at: **international.cengage.com/region**

Cengage Learning products are represented in Canada by Nelson Education, Ltd.

Visit National Geographic Learning online at **ngl.cengage.com**

Visit our corporate website at **www.cengage.com**

Photo credits

The publishers would like to thank the following sources for permission to reproduce their copyright protected photographs:

Cover photo: (John Burcham/National Geographic Image Collection)

pp 5 (Panoramic Images/National Geographic Image Collection), 6 (wessley/Shutterstock), 6 (KERVELLA rafy/Shutterstock), 6 (digitalskillet/iStockphoto.com), 6 (Ashwin82/iStockphoto.com), 6 (alynst/iStockphoto.com), 6 (Shutterstock), 7 (Christopher Futcher), 8 (Marilyn Volan/Shutterstock), 8 (Adrian Sherratt/Alamy), 8 (EmmanuelD/Fotolia.com), 9 (Shutterstock.com), 10 (Shutterstock.com), 10 (Shutterstock.com), 12 (Shutterstock.com), 13 (Penny Tweedie/Corbis), 13 (Fancy/photolibrary.uk.com), 14 (Shutterstock.com), 14 (Benedict Allen), 14 (Shutterstock.com), 14 (Shutterstock.com), 14 (Shutterstock.com), 14 (Shutterstock.com), 14 (Shutterstock.com), 14 (Shutterstock.com), 15 (Medford Taylor/National Geographic Image Collection), 16 (Shutterstock.com), 16 (Denise Truscello/Gettyimages.co.uk), 16 (David Alan Harvey/National Geographic Image Collection), 16 (Shutterstock.com), 18 (Shutterstock.com), 18 (Shutterstock.com), 19 (Shutterstock.com), 19 (Ferenc Szelepcsenyi/Alamy), 19 (Hee Chul Kim/Gettyimages.co.uk), 20 (Shutterstock.com), 20 (Shutterstock.com), 20 (Shutterstock.com), 20 (Shutterstock.com), 20 (Shutterstock.com), 20 (Shutterstock.com), 20 (Shutterstock.com), 20 (Shutterstock.com), 21 (Shutterstock.com), 21 (Shutterstock.com), 21 (Shutterstock.com), 22 (Cooter/Alamy), 22 (Prudence Cuming Associates/Handout/Reuters/Corbis), 22-23 (MikeShannon/BigStockPhoto.com), 23 (Alexander Burkatovski/Corbis), 23 (World History Archive/Alamy), 24 (Shutterstock.com), 24 (Shutterstock.com), 27 (Shutterstock.com), 28 (Shutterstock.com), 29 (James P. Blair/National Geographic Image Collection), 30 (Shutterstock.com), 30 (Mark Thiessen/National Geographic Image Collection), 30 (Shutterstock.com), 30 (Norbert Wu/Minden Pictures/National Geographic Image Collection), 32 (Shutterstock.com), 32 (Shutterstock.com), 32 (Shutterstock.com), 33 (Shutterstock.com), 34 (Shutterstock.com), 34 (Shutterstock.com), 35 (Vidura Luis Barrios/Alamy), 36 (John Stanmeyer/National Geographic Image Collection), 36 (Dabjola/BigStockPhoto.com), 36 (Shutterstock.com), 37 (Mooneyphoto/Malaria No More/Press Association Images), 37 (Shutterstock.com), 37 (Shutterstock.com), 37 (Shutterstock.com), 38 (Shutterstock.com), 38 (Pascal Le Segretain/Sygma/Corbis), 39 (Carsten Peter/National Geographic Image Collection), 40 (Shutterstock.com), 40 (Shutterstock.com), 40 (Shutterstock.com), 42 (Shutterstock.com), 42 (Raymond Gehman/National Geographic Image Collection), 44 (Shutterstock.com), 44 (Shutterstock.com), 44 (Shutterstock.com), 45 (David Hughes/123rf.com), 46 (littledutchgirl/iStockphoto.com), 46 (Patricio Robles Gil/Minden Pictures/National Geographic Image Collection), 47 (Ravet007/iStockphoto.com), 47 (Shutterstock.com), 48 (Shutterstock.com), 52 (Shutterstock.com), 52 (Shutterstock.com), 53 (Randy Olson/National Geographic Image Collection), 54 (digitalskillet/iStockphoto.com), 54 (Shutterstock.com), 54 (Shutterstock.com), 54 (Shutterstock.com), 56 (Shutterstock.com), 56 (Shutterstock.com), 56 (Shutterstock.com), 56 (Shutterstock.com), 56 (Shutterstock.com), 59 (WinterWitch/iStockphoto.com), 60 (SteveRosset/iStockphoto.com), 60 (Randy Olson/National Geographic Image Collection), 62 (Shutterstock.com), 62 (Tim Laman/National Geographic Image Collection), 63 (Mark Thiessen/National Geographic Image Collection), 64 (Paramount Television/The Kobal Collection/www.picture-desk.com), 64 (Shutterstock.com), 64 (Shutterstock.com), 66 (Shutterstock.com), 66 (Reuters/Issei Kato), 66 (Jim Richardson/National Geographic Image Collection), 70 (Harveys Art/BigStockPhoto.com), 70 (2000adonline.com), 70 (Hodder & Stoughton), 71 (Shutterstock.com), 71 (Shutterstock.com), 76 (Shutterstock.com), 76 (Shutterstock.com), 77 (Jodi Cobb/National Geographic Image Collection), 78 (Shutterstock.com), 78 (Shutterstock.com), 78 (Imagine/Universal/The Kobal Collection/Reed, Eli), 78 (Mirisch-7 Arts/United Artists/The Kobal Collection/www.picture-desk.com), 78 (Paramount/The Kobal Collection), 79 (Shutterstock.com), 80-81 (Shutterstock.com), 80-81 (European Youth Parliament), 81 (Shutterstock.com), 81 (Shutterstock.com), 84 (Frans Lemmens/Gettyimages.co.uk), 84 (mbousquet/iStockphoto.com), 85 (Tim Graham/The Image Bank/Gettyimages.co.uk), 85 (The Prince's Trust), 86 (Shutterstock.com), 86 (Shutterstock.com), 86 (Shutterstock.com), 86 (Shutterstock.com), 86 (Shutterstock.com), 86 (Shutterstock.com), 86 (Shutterstock.com), 87 (George F. Mobley/National Geographic Image Collection), 88 (Carsten Peter/National Geographic Image Collection), 88 (Shutterstock.com), 88 (Shutterstock.com), 89 (David Mclain/National Geographic Image Collection), 89 (Paul Sutherland/National Geographic Image Collection), 90-91 (Shutterstock.com), 90-91 (Shutterstock.com), 90-91 (Shutterstock.com), 90-91 (Shutterstock.com), 91 (Vasiliki Christoforidou/NewEd Design), 93 (Shutterstock.com), 94 (Cotton Coulson/National Geographic Image Collection), 94 (Brian J. Skerry/National Geographic Image Collection), 94 (Bill Gentile/Corbis), 100 (Shutterstock.com), 100 (Shutterstock.com), 100 (Shutterstock.com), 100 (Shutterstock.com), 100 (Shutterstock.com), 109 (Shutterstock.com), 110 (Shutterstock.com), 111 (Shutterstock.com), 112 (Shutterstock.com), 113 (Shutterstock.com), 114 (Shutterstock.com), 115 (Shutterstock.com), 116 (Shutterstock.com)

Illustrations by Mark Draisey pp 31, 55; Mark Duffin p 71; Celia Hart pp 26, 61, 95, 97, 98; Eric Smith pp 17, 25, 49, 65, 69, 73, 97; Laszlo Veres pp 50, 74, 98

Printed in Greece by Bakis sa
Print Number: 08 Print Year: 2018